11.99

Three Years

In The Alaskan Bush

Colleen T. Weber

Copyright © 2007 Colleen T. Weber
All rights reserved.
ISBN: 1-4196-6274-0
ISBN-13: 978-1419662744

Visit www.booksurge.com to order additional copies.

Three Years

This book is dedicated to my aunt Theresa who kept us in chocolate and other goodies while we were so isolated from our family and loved ones.

She never missed a holiday.

She also saved all of my letters so that I might use them for this book.

PROLOGUE

Like a large bird scouting the terrain below, the small plane swooped down toward a single, large building, flew directly over the roof and lazily circled toward the end of the short gravel runway. As I anticipated the landing, one question kept going through my mind, *What am I doing in this forsaken, barren tundra?* Unbidden, tears welled up and a huge lump caught in my throat. I quickly glanced back at my two children. For their sakes I knew I must remain calm, so took two deep breaths.

The pilot turned to me, "We had to let them know we were here. That's why I buzzed the school. Hope it didn't frighten you."

I nodded, indicating that it hadn't. *At least not too badly*, I thought.

As we landed, I saw two small boats pull up to the shore only a few feet from the runway. As soon as the pilot stopped the plane he jumped out, walked around, opened our doors and helped each of us to the ground. As we deplaned, the two boatmen approached. One was a huge, muscular African American with so much gold dangling from his neck and ears my first thought was, *He could pass for Mr. T*. The second man was smaller than his partner—slender with straight black hair and a scruffy mustache. We had just landed in Tuntutuliak, Alaska, a small village of Yup'ik Eskimos where I was to teach for the next nine months.

Everything happened so quickly I hardly had time to take it in. First, the larger of the two men introduced himself as Hunter. He then introduced the smaller man as James, the maintenance man for the school. Since the pilot already knew the men, he wasted no time on pleasantries and immediately began handing out boxes and bags. The children and I helped carry our things to the waiting boats where Hunter and James skillfully packed them.

I told the pilot thank you as he prepared to leave while the children stood watching, fascinated, as Hunter and James finished their task. When everything was stowed in the boats to the men's satisfaction Hunter directed each of us to our places where we literally had to squeeze in amongst the boxes and bags. Soon we were moving down the Knak River towards the BIA School, which was only a short distance away.

Once the boats were docked everyone grabbed something to carry. We were escorted into the school, down a hall and into the teacher's quarters, which were located in the northwest corner of the school building. As my children and I entered the apartment I was relieved to see that the many boxes we had sent earlier with our food, clothes and household items, had arrived safely. With Hunter and James help, we finished unloading the boats and added these boxes and bags to the stacks already in the apartment that was to be our home for the next nine months.

Tuntutuliak Grade School is the old part to the right. Our apartment is the newer section to the left. My classroom was located behind the three windows just to the left of the stairs.

Upon our arrival we had given our living quarters only a cursory glance, as we were busy unloading the boats. As I checked over the boxes I was pleased to see all our sent-ahead things had arrived. We now proceeded to explore the apartment and I was pleased to find that we had running water, a washer and dryer and a complete bathroom, as I had heard stories of honey buckets. (It wasn't until later we learned the school had the *only* running water in the entire village and about a year later that we were introduced to the "honey bucket".) Although we had running water, our toilet would prove to be an almost constant source of irritation the entire time we were there—mainly because it was a recyclable system that wasn't very efficient—or good smelling!

Once the boats had been unloaded and the apartment explored, the kids asked to explore the village. By then I was both emotionally and physically exhausted, and I needed some quiet time to unpack and organize my thoughts as well as our belongings. After remonstrating with John to keep a close watch over Anne, I let them go.

Alone for a time, my thoughts began to go back over the events which led to this time and place. I still couldn't believe all that had happened in the past to get us here. As I unpacked my mind drifted back...

Ron and I grew up in a small town in SE Washington where we'd known each other since grade school. We'd gone through high school together as good friends. After graduation Ron joined the marines for four years but was discharged in early 1965 when he smashed his leg while bull riding one weekend on base.

While Ron was in the Marines I attended college and we kept in close contact. I received my teaching degree and graduated on August 8, 1965. Eight days later we were married and two weeks after that I began teaching school in our hometown of Touchet, Washington.

Growing up, one of my main goals in life was to get married and have a family, but sometimes things don't go as planned. During my freshman year in college I was diagnosed with ovarian cysts which became such a severe problem that eventually I had to have both ovaries removed. It was hard to accept the fact that I could never have children, but soon that seemed only a minor obstacle as I figured we could always adopt.

After Ron and I had been married several years we decided to proceed with adoption but were surprised to find that we couldn't adopt unless we owned our own home. Not long after that Ron's parents sold their farm, and we bought the house and thirteen acres. We were on our way to qualifying for a child!

We remodeled the house and naturally, one of the rooms became, "the baby's room." I was then in my ninth year of teaching and Ron had gotten a full time job. His leg held him back for a while and then he spent several years working part time for different farmers.

Everything was falling into place, and in January of 1974, we filled out the paperwork for adoption. At that time we also found that the rules had changed. I could continue working and we could still adopt. We requested, as our first choice, a baby but did say we would consider an older child. Since I had decided I didn't want to work fulltime if we got a baby, I submitted my resignation for the following year.

In late March we received "the call!" It wasn't a baby, but it was a child—a five and a half year old little boy named John who needed a home. After discussing it we made plans to have him visit us a couple weekends. He lived in town and Ron feared he might have trouble adjusting to farm life.

Three days before we were to meet with him for the first time, I received another call from the adoption agency. John had been sent away from his foster home and had nowhere to go. They asked if we could take him NOW!

I called Ron to discuss the situation. We made arrangements to get John the next day. We picked him up at the home of the man who ran the adoption agency. On the way home John wore us out talking and asking questions. When we showed him around the house he decided he wanted to sleep in the baby's room, which was closer to our room. Ron nixed that. He felt it wouldn't be a good idea. If we eventually did get a baby John might resent being moved to another room.

The next morning when we awoke we found John rummaging through every drawer and cupboard in the kitchen. He had not had this type of freedom in the past and was a very curious youngster.

I still had several months of school left and the adoption agency felt it would be in John's best interest to stay enrolled in the Head Start Program in Walla Walla. Each morning Ron took him to school. Ron's mother would pick him up at noon and take him to her house. Then Ron would bring him home after work.

It didn't take long for things to deteriorate. John was constantly in trouble at school and wouldn't mind Ron's mom.

Being first-time parents and starting with a troubled five-year-old, we didn't know what do but were trying our best.

After we had been struggling along with John for several weeks, we got a second call from the adoption agency. This time it was a baby girl. Naturally I wanted this child, as I had waited impatiently for a baby and felt this was the moment. On the other hand, Ron was hesitant and didn't want another child right then, especially a baby, because the situation with John had turned out to be extremely frustrating. But I talked Ron into at least going to Spokane to see the baby.

Anne was almost a month old by the time we got the call because her mother had been uncertain about giving her up—at least that was what we were told. We couldn't visit her right away because Ron, John and I all had the flue and the adoption agency didn't want her exposed to the bug.

Finally, we were well and on our way to Spokane. I was terribly excited, but Ron kept telling me to wait until we at least saw the baby before we made any decisions. His reasoning was that Anne was Native American and he was concerned she would feel "different" growing up in our little town.

My sister warned us that an adoptive child came with only a diaper. If we decided to take the baby we would need to have clothes to take her home, so I went prepared.

We arrived at the agency and were ushered into a small room where we waited for them to bring Anne to us. As soon as I saw her my heart melted. She was all dressed in pink. They had tried to plaster her beautiful black hair down, but strands were already sticking straight out of the tiny pink bows they had tied in it.

When they placed her in my arms, I took one look and knew I couldn't let go of her. We had explained to John where we were going and why. When I showed him the baby he started bouncing up and down he was so excited about having a baby sister. Ron was the only one who remained reserved, but he agreed to take her.

The agency representative said she must take Anne back to take off the clothes. I had a terrible time relinquishing her for even a few minutes. Sure enough, just as my sister had predicted, when Anne was returned to my arms she was clad in only a diaper. I immediately dressed her in the outfit we had fortunately brought with us.

I couldn't wait to show her to my sister and her family who were waiting outside, but first the paperwork had to be signed. Once that was finished I proudly showed our new daughter off to her relatives. We headed for home after everyone had ooohed and aaahed over her. At home we finally had a baby for our baby room, and I now thought I had it all.

There was only a month of school left so Ron's mom came to stay with us to care for both children while I was at work. Although she was a great help with the children, I was anxious to take over and thought the month would never end. Finally school was out! I was now home with our little family. It didn't take long to find out that taking care of a new baby and a 5 1/2 year old was NOT easy! Fortunately my younger brother spent the summer with us. When he wasn't working he would help watch the kids, which gave me time to get things done around our little farm.

In my idyllic thoughts I had planned to can fruit and prepare for the next winter as much as possible. I wouldn't be working, so our income would be cut in half. Ron would be the sole provider, something that had never happened before in our marriage. My income had always been consistent and usually the larger of the two.

Although I did make an effort, and with my mother-in-law and brother helping with the children, I was at least able to put away a few jars of fruit and jam, but it was definitely not an easy task with a tiny baby! And I certainly didn't near reach my goal!

In September when school started, John entered kindergarten in the local school. In the morning he rode the school bus, then I picked him up at noon. Each day I dressed Anne in a cute little dress when we went to get John. While she soon gained the reputation of a little doll and everyone loved her, John developed his own reputation—but it was not all positive. He wouldn't mind the teachers and was constantly getting into trouble.

In October we received a third call from the adoption agency about a three-year-old boy. This time I was the one who hesitated but decided to at least tell Ron of the call. I had already decided that I couldn't raise another baby. Even though I dearly loved Anne, I hadn't realized that raising a tiny baby was so stressful. I knew I did not want to go through that again.

I called Ron at work and told him of the agency's call. I assumed he wouldn't be interested. I told him how I felt about raising a baby. To my surprise he said he would like another son.

Once again we were on our way to Spokane's adoption agency. Brad was a darling little three-year-old, and both Ron and I were attracted to him immediately. For some reason, Brad became extremely attached to Ron. One day while Brad was napping, my brother came by and asked Ron and John to go hunting with him and his son. When Brad woke up he asked me, "Where is daddy?"

I told him, "Everyone has gone hunting."

His response was, "If everyone is hunting, why am I still here with you!" I didn't have an answer to that one.

Now the fun really began. Unfortunately John hadn't had any of the childhood diseases most children get before age five or six. Shortly after Brad arrived John brought home the measles. Brad was next and Anne followed. Chicken pox, mumps and pink eye followed the measles in rapid succession, and on New Year's Eve we were just finishing up the last of these childhood diseases.

By now Ron's check was our only income, and he was beginning to show signs of strain over our situation. He would come home late, sit in his chair and stare. Sometimes he would brag about driving home at exceedingly high speeds.

Things weren't getting any better with John, while Ron was overwhelmed with the responsibility of totally supporting a family of five and dealing with John's difficulties. In February Ron suddenly said he couldn't handle our situation anymore and Brad had to go back. I was devastated because Brad was such a superb little guy, and he and Anne had become close. Ron's reasoning was that John might not find another permanent home whereas Brad would. Even though I was inconsolable and couldn't deal with losing Brad, Ron was adamant. He packed up Brad and his belongings and took him back to Spokane. That day something inside of me died. I was losing a child I had grown to love as my own. One who had truly become my son.

Now things got worse. I discovered Ron had been hanging around a lady at the office for some time. When we finally met she learned Ron had been lying about our relationship so she applied for a transfer and moved.

I thought Ron's and my relationship might be better now and for a while it appeared to be. Anne was a little doll and attached to her dad. Whenever we stopped by his work everyone would fuss over her. Ron enjoyed this attention.

In contrast, John was having more and more problems. He didn't mind, he lied, told whopper stories, and Ron wanted him to play sports, which was a total disaster.

We started spending more time with Ron's youngest brother and his family. Ron's sister-in-law was never my favorite person, yet Ron began spending time with her discussing their problems.

About that time we got word that my brother, who lived in Redmond, Oregon, was going to sing a solo in a big high school music concert. My sister Julie, her three kids, my grandfather, and my two kids and I decided to attend. Since I drove a large station wagon it was decided everyone would ride with me. Our plan had been to drive to Redmond, attended the concert on Friday night and stay with my parents until Sunday. We attended the concert as planned, but Saturday evening my aunt called to tell my grandfather that his best friend had died. Grandpa was so devastated that he wanted to go home immediately! Since we couldn't convince him to stay until the next day my sister and I quickly packed up and headed home.

WHAT A TRIP! There were five tired kids in the back of the station wagon. John tormented Anne who would scream. In turn I yelled at John. Julie didn't say anything on the trip, but when we got to her house five hours later I realized how furious she was. She chastised me about spoiling Anne and blaming John. She was right, but I was too tired to care.

By the time I dropped my grandfather at his house it was well after midnight. He wanted me to stay the night at his house, but the kids were asleep and I just wanted to go home.

Finally arriving home I lifted a sleeping Anne out of her car seat and also supported John as we walked into the house. First I got him to bed. As I was carrying Anne through the kitchen to her room, I noticed a purse. I went into the living room and saw glasses and cigarette butts on the coffee table. After putting Anne to bed, I walked toward our room and was met by Ron. I thought he was acting strange as he went into the kitchen. For some reason I didn't follow him but walked into our room where I saw his sister-in-law hiding behind our bed...naked.

I was furious! I went back to the kitchen, grabbed her purse, threw it across the room spilling the contents and yelling, "Explain what the hell is going on!"

Ron told how Karen had been bugging him for months to have sex with her. (Of course he could have declined!) I had known she always wanted whatever I had, but I hadn't realized that included my husband. Of course, Ron promised to stay away from her and asked for another chance. Since I had been reared a strict Catholic and didn't believe in divorce I figured we could work through anything. Ron assured me he really didn't want to lose his family. He had just wanted to "have his cake and eat it, too," as he put it.

While I was talking with Ron Karen simply got dressed and called her husband to come get her. I have no idea what story she told him, but the next day when he called as if nothing had happened I was not very nice before hanging up the phone. (I was still very angry!)

After that, Karen kept calling the house pestering us and eventually even threatened us. When that happened we took the children to another of Ron's brother's and went into town to try to reason with her. She had the audacity to tell us to leave or she'd call the police. Her husband was out of town at the time. We couldn't talk to him so we went home and hoped she'd forget her threat. (She did.)

Time passed and things seemed to get better. Then Ron started hanging around another young woman at the office. When I found out I asked him to go to counseling as I still hoped we could work things out to save our marriage. Unfortunately for us, our counselor was a divorcee who was living with a much younger man.

The way I figured it she probably felt better about herself knowing Ron was in a similar situation because after only a couple of sessions he came home and announced, "The counselor has recommended I leave you." With that he began packing and prepared to move in with his mother.

As he was packing, I called the counselor and asked, "What gave you the authority to make a decision about what should happen in our marriage?"

She flippantly responded, "One day you will thank me."

My response isn't printable.

Ron later told me that as he was leaving he almost changed his mind when Anne ran down the driveway crying, "Please came back, Daddy!"

He said, "I was afraid that if I did go back, I wouldn't leave at all."

When we got a legal separation Ron wanted the farm, the furniture and about everything else we owned. He did take what little savings we had and bought me some used furniture at an auction. The children and I moved into the small community where I rented a house from my aunt and uncle.

I didn't object to Ron keeping the farm and the house because a friend of mine had kept her farm after the divorce and I'd seen the adverse affects of her trying to keep up a place by herself. I decided that wasn't for me.

Although I had substitute taught during the past six years, I hadn't worked full time. Now I needed a full time job. I went to our school to see if anything was available. They didn't have an opening for the following school year but did have a teaching position open for summer school. I accepted the job.

As the past few years had had an adverse affect on me, I went in to talk to the man who ran the adoption agency for some advice. After listening to my story he told me, "You're falling to pieces. If you don't get away from Ron and this situation you won't be any good to the kids or yourself."

What he said frightened me. I packed my bags and headed to Redmond, Oregon, to spend a few weeks with my parents before summer school started. Later, my parents told me that I must have been extremely exhausted from all of the stress because I slept for several days upon my arrival.

My sister was studying to become a teacher so I asked her to come back with me and help teach summer school. She agreed. As soon as summer school was out in August I packed everything and moved with the children to Redmond. There we moved into a small trailer owned by my parents. My dad rented the trailer to me for $75.00 per month since I wasn't working. My only income was $75.00 per month for each child plus $300.00 a month for my share of our farm. $450.00 a month didn't go far when trying to support three people.

Shortly after our marriage broke up, I began inquiring into teaching positions in other areas, especially Alaska. I had heard you could make more money teaching in Alaska than in Washington. I found an advertisement requesting teachers for remote Eskimo villages along the Kuskokwim River out of

Bethel. I made a phone call and was fortunate to contact Cal Lundy. He told me what was required to teach in Alaska. I began taking college classes to earn teaching certificates for both Oregon and Alaska as I was still certified in Washington. I sent out fifty or sixty applications to various areas of Washington and Oregon, but didn't get even *one* interview. I realized this might be partly because I hadn't been teaching full time for the past six years.

I continued to communicate with Cal for almost a year after our initial contact. Finally in January of 1980, he called me about an opening for the BIA out of Bethel, Alaska. (The BIA is the Bureau of Indian Affairs run by the Federal Government.)

Having been a total washout as a waitress I had taken over a private kindergarten when Cal called me about the job. I was hesitant to walk out on my students. While still mulling over the job offer, Cal called back to say that President Johnson had put a freeze on all government hiring. I would have to wait.

I continued on with my kindergarten. Anne was then in first grade doing an excellent job. John was in fifth grade not doing as well. He had taken on a paper route, but would only collect for the paper when he needed money, many times not delivering the papers. When I found out I made him pay the people back and quit the job, but school was still a daily struggle.

In May of that same year I received "The Letter!" Cal was coming to Oregon and suggested I come for an interview. Since my two sisters also had teaching degrees and were looking for work I called and asked Cal if the three of us could come together. He said, "Sure."

We went for a group interview. After that whenever one of us talked to him he would refer to us as "one of the three sisters". (At least we made an impression and he didn't forget us!)

A few weeks later Cal called offering me a job in Tuntutuliak, Alaska. He also offered a job to one of my sisters, but it was in a different village. She didn't want to be alone in a remote village and had just been offered a job in Canby, Oregon, so she declined. My other sister was a PE/Health teacher and Cal didn't have any openings for her at that time.

Now the work really began. I was sent a list of what I would need for the year, both food and supplies. Everything had to be shipped airmail and each of the boxes could be no larger than an apple box. I was also limited in the total number of pounds I could send.

I spent the rest of the summer collecting the needed supplies. It seemed as if I dried boxes and boxes of apples and other fruit. Other staples recommended were powdered eggs, powdered milk, and flour. Besides food, we were given specific guidelines regarding extra warm winter clothes including "mud boots" for spring and fall. (Mud boots are "almost knee-high" rubber boots.)

The time was almost here for the children and I to leave. I had shipped out most of our supplies and the BIA had purchased our tickets to fly to the school. The agreement with the BIA was if we didn't stay a full year I had to refund the cost of the airline tickets. If we stayed two years, they would give us tickets to fly back home. Still, it cost me almost $1000 of my own money to buy and ship the supplies we would need for the year.

I was informed that there *was* a small store in the village but not to count on any particular items being there. You could only buy what they had, not what you wanted, and both fresh fruit and canned goods were extremely high priced...if and when they were available.

Finally the time arrived to leave for Alaska. By now my sister Cindy had settled in Canby, Oregon, so I packed our carryons and the three of us went to stay with her before leaving. The temperature that August in Canby was over 100 degrees and Cindy didn't have air conditioning. I unpacked the things I thought would melt or spoil and put them in her refrigerator for the night.

The plan was for the children and I to stay with Cindy the first night. We would all go to my aunt and uncle's home the next night as they lived near the Portland airport. Cindy would take us to the airport early in the morning. My aunt and uncle had air conditioning so it was much cooler that night. Still I unpacked the margarine and refrigerated it. I wanted the assurance it would make it to the airport without melting.

The morning of our departure we headed for the Portland airport bright and early. At that time you could take several items for each person, then pay seven dollars for each additional box or suitcase. With the three of us it added up to a car full. We unloaded the bags and boxes and moved them into the line at the Wien Air counter.

Finally, it was my turn to get rid of our baggage. The attendant cheerfully checked in box after box until she came to one of the last boxes. She noticed something dripping from the bottom and said it couldn't be shipped that way. For a moment I panicked, but she calmly told me to take the box into the central area, take out whatever was leaking, repack the box and bring it back. She even gave me a roll of tape to reseal the box. I sighed and thought, *One more hurdle to overcome.*

Nerves taut and close to tears, I dragged the box into the center of the airport. As I began unpacking I heard the kids yell, "Daddy!" Looking up I saw Ron approaching. He had decided to come see the kids off since it would be at least nine months before he saw them again. While he took the children aside, I proceeded to deal with the leaky box.

At the very bottom of the box I found one pound of margarine I'd missed when refrigerating items the two previous nights. Fortunately I had wrapped the margarine in plastic so the damage was minimal. Carefully I carried the greasy mess to the trash container and deposited it. Now my hands were covered with grease. As I stood there frantically searching around the lobby for something with which to clean them my sister suggested I relax and she would get some paper towels from the restroom. After I'd cleaned up and repacked the box I took it back to the counter where the lady inspected it and sent it down the conveyor belt. *One more problem solved.*

When it was time to board, the children and I said our goodbyes to their dad and Aunt Cindy. With waves and brave smiles we boarded the plane that would take us to our new lives in a totally new environment.

It seemed we had hardly gotten seated when an announcement came. "Ladies and gentlemen: there is an airline pilot's strike which means you will have to stay in the plane while we wait our turn to depart. You will not be able to deplane as we have to be ready to leave at a moment's notice."

Of course all the children soon became bored. The airline wanted to keep the customers as contented as possible so they had the hostesses provide cards, pop, peanuts and toy wings to keep the kids busy and entertained. I spent the next couple of hours playing card games, reading and coloring as I also had packed things for them to do anticipating a long flight—just not this long!

After almost two hours waiting on a stationary plane the announcement finally came. We took off for Seattle where we had to go through the same routine again. After another long wait we headed to Anchorage. Fortunately the planes in Anchorage were flying so there was only a short delay before taking off for Bethel.

We arrived in Bethel over four hours late so it was well after midnight when we deplaned. There was only one person at the airport—a car rental lady who was just preparing to leave as we entered the terminal. Quickly, I rushed over to ask her for help. When she realized I was a teacher she made a phone call, told me someone would be there shortly, and left.

Now we were all alone in a strange airport several thousand miles from home. The kids were utterly exhausted and I was completely drained. We had no choice but to wait. About twenty minutes later an extremely polite gentleman arrived. Even though he couldn't find our names on his list, he helped us pack everything but one suitcase in the storage room at the airport. (We had been told to plan one suitcase for the overnight stay in Bethel.) He then took us to a dorm-like building where he had the night crew to set us up with a room.

I tried to tell him I thought we were supposed to be staying at the Kuskokwim Inn but he only replied, "No, all new teachers stay here before being sent to a village."

Since I was in no condition to argue I put the kids to bed immediately upon being assigned a room. They promptly fell asleep. It took a while longer for my nerves to relax enough to sleep.

About three in the morning I awoke to a knock on my window. I looked up and saw a man on the ledge trying to get in. He signaled for me to open the window and without thinking I actually got up and tried, but the window was sealed shut. I yelled through the window that it wouldn't open. Then I went back to bed.

At 8:00 the next morning I was to meet with the personnel lady. I got up and dressed but left the kids sleeping. Once in the hall I looked for someone to tell about the man at the window. The worker there said, "That's really strange. This morning we found a man sleeping on the couch in the waiting room down the hall. But what we can't figure out is how he got in there. We are on the second floor. Everything was locked up and there is no way he could have climbed up from outside."

I didn't know how the man had done it, but was sure I hadn't imagined the man outside my window in the middle of the night.

The worker directed me to the personnel office. When I entered the lady in charge asked my name and started looking for my file. While she was looking I told her about the man at the window and she just brushed it off saying, "No one could have climbed up there from the outside." (Later. I actually checked it out myself. I couldn't see how he had gotten up there, but I knew for sure I hadn't imagined seeing a man at my window and felt certain he was the same man that had been found asleep on the couch that morning.)

Finally the lady turned to me and said, "I have searched all our files and have nothing on you. Let me take a look in the other room."

I sat there trying not to panic but thinking depressing thoughts, *I've spent most of my money getting here. Everything we own is either sitting in Tuntutuliak or here and I don't have enough money left to get us home, much less all of our belongings.*

Soon she returned, "Still nothing," she said. She sat there a moment contemplating, then asked, "Who hired you?"

When I told her Cal Lundy had hired me she smiled, shook her head, picked up the phone and dialed a number. I couldn't figure out what was going on.

"Hey Cal," she said into the phone, "you missing a teacher over there?" She listened for a few seconds then laughed as she said, "Okay," hung up the phone and turned towards me. "You were hired by the BIA, and we're the Lower Kuskowkwim School District, which is the state system. Cal will send someone for you in about an hour. Meanwhile you lucked out. We charge teachers $15.00 a night and the Kuskokwim Inn charges $68.00. We are also much cleaner and safer." She laughed again as she said, "It was nice meeting you. If you decide to work for the state, come see me!"

I paid her, went upstairs, packed, and got the kids dressed. Then we went downstairs to wait for our ride.

Phyllis, the lady that came to get us, was super. She took us to the BIA complex. In the parking lot I was fascinated to see what looked like a "hitching rail" with extension cords wrapped around it and outlets hanging from the cords. When I asked her about them she explained that in winter you plugged your vehicle into the outlets to keep the oil from freezing. She then pointed out the plug extending from the front of her car. (Several years later I would also have a vehicle that needed to be plugged into an electrical outlet during the winter.)

She took the kids to her apartment inside the bureau offices and had them join her family for breakfast, then led me to Cal's office. Cal was a big jolly fellow who got quite a kick out of the fact that the state school system had to get up in the middle of the night to take care of us; not the BIA.

I completed what seemed like a ream of paperwork, got fingerprinted and the three of us were hustled out to the airport to retrieve our belongings. Amazing as it may seem, I had remained <u>fairly</u> calm and collected through everything that had happened the past twenty-four hours. As we approached the ticket counter, Phyllis asked me to get our tickets for the final leg of our journey. So much had happened I couldn't remember where I put them and PANICKED! Frantically I started searching everywhere at the same time! As she led me to a chair Phyllis said sternly, "Sit down, calm down and think."

With tears in my eyes I sat down, took some deep breaths and methodically searched, and eventually found, the tickets in my carry-on bag—just where they should have been. I remember thinking, *At least our plane is a charter so it won't leave without us!*

It took a while to load everything we had, but eventually we were all packed into the little charter plane. We took off and headed for our new home. As the plane rose over the tundra I was awestruck by the view. There were miles and miles of flat land covered with lakes, rivers and slews. Actually, it looked more like huge lakes, rivers and slews surrounded by smaller amounts of land!

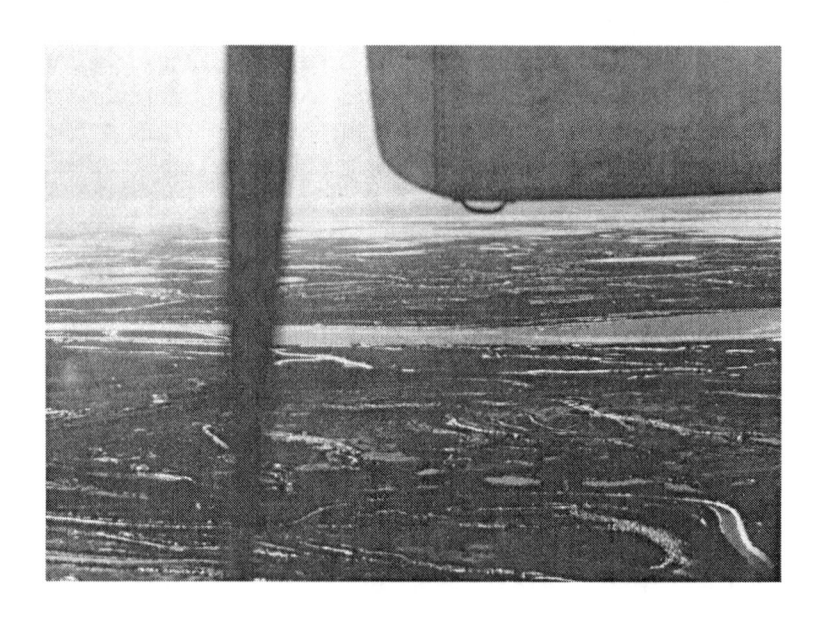

A view of the tundra flying out of Bethel

We had spent over eighteen hours on airplanes to get to our new home, and now we were here with the next nine months looming ahead. I knew we couldn't even think about leaving before the year was out. I just didn't have the money. I took a break from unpacking and sat down as I remembered an old saying I had once heard, "This is the first day of the rest of your life..."

Year One

By the time John and Anne returned with excited stories about the kids and the different activities they had witnessed in the village, I had done quite a lot of unpacking—at least as far as finding the bedding and more essential necessities for that night. John eagerly told of learning about all the areas where one shouldn't step off the boardwalk and how he was planning to take me around the next day and show me. It made me feel somewhat better when I heard the children's enthusiasm.

We ate supper with the Hunters and I learned more about the village, the school and in general what the year would be like. Sharon was to be my principal while her husband, whom everyone just called Hunter, would be supervising her as she was still working on her principal's credentials. Hunter also taught grades six, seven, and eight. I would be teaching ESL (English as a second language) to the third grade and regular classes to grades four and five. Native teachers would teach grades one, two and three, with Sharon teaching that ESL.

The next morning the children and I finished unpacking and while I cleaned the kitchen and living room they helped put things away. That afternoon I went with them, as they were eager to help me explore the village. Lower village was made up of about twenty houses that were connected to each other by a boardwalk. The people living there were mainly of the Moravian religion.

One of the first things explained to us was the purpose of the walkway. I never did know for sure if the explanation was accurate, but we took it seriously. We were told that to step off the walkway could have serious consequences. Evidently the ground was so soggy that one might sink into the muddy soil. The weeds could also be deceiving as they could be covering a sinkhole where you might disappear into the depths. To whomever had explained this to John and Anne the day before, I was very thankful as they had accepted the seriousness of the situation and John was right there to show me each place he thought was dangerous as we passed through the village.

The setup of the village was rather unique, as there were several lakes in the village itself and another just to the east of the schoolhouse. Across this lake was where Cooperation Store was located. To get there one had to follow the boardwalk around the village: no shortcuts. Cooperation Store carried village essentials such as pop, sugar cereals and candy.

The fire station is to the left and Corporation Store to the right. The lake is directly behind our apartment.

It didn't take long to figure out that if I went to Cooperation Store right after a delivery I might get frozen meat, not very fresh vegetables and eggs. But each dozen eggs usually contained five or six "green" eggs that were so old they had a green tinge to them and had to be thrown out.

In our exploration that day we found there were two other small stores in the village. One was in the front of a family's home while the other was located in a small section of the airline building.

Two other important buildings were the clinic and the government office. The government office housed the village telephone. It was explained to me that if I wanted to make a phone call I would go to the office, stand in line until my turn came, write down the time and number I was calling, step up to the phone and make my call. In the event I was actually able to get a call through, I learned quickly that I should warn the party I was calling that the phone might cut out at any time so we needed to get the most important business or news exchanged first. At the end of each month I would be given a bill for my calls. A couple of months after we arrived a small enclosure was built around the phone so people could talk somewhat privately while those waiting their turns were outside the "phone booth" in the office.

Next we went to Upper Village, which consisted of ten to twelve homes, a tiny Greek Orthodox Church and a new, four-million-dollar, state-run high school with a gym. Upper Village was around the bend of the Knak River only a short walk from Lower Village.

One of the first things I noticed about the village was the smell of fish. Many homes had racks on their roofs and it was interesting to see fish hanging from these racks. It was disturbing though to see the masses of flies that covered the fish.

At first I wondered why the houses were built off the ground. Later I learned that in the fall when the river overflowed the water went under the houses near the river and didn't damage them. I also found out that the river was constantly breaking down the bank in the curve right below the BIA schoolhouse where I taught. It was expected that in a few more years the school would be at the bottom of the river. (And that is exactly where it is now.)

Another interesting thing I learned was that Tuntutuliak was a "dry" village. That meant liquor wasn't allowed in the village. Of course that didn't stop all of the drinking, but at least this village was trying to address the alcohol problem.

My uncle had warned us about the "no-see-ems". They were tiny gnat-like insects with a bad little sting. Fortunately we had brought some aloe vera with us. It helped keep the itching under control.

We discovered right away that the village kids loved to visit. The toilet also intrigued them, and it was constantly in need of draining and cleaning. Our apartment became a popular hangout—at least for a while.

Saturday, the fourth day we were in the village, John went hunting with his friend Peter. They got into a beehive and both came home with stings. Thank goodness again for aloe vera as it helped relieve the pain and take down the swelling. One of Peter's stings had been right at the corner of his eye, which had almost swollen shut. After applying aloe vera we could actually watch the swelling recede.

I started cleaning and organizing my classroom in preparation for the first day of school. When I was told I couldn't keep Anne with me after school I was pretty upset, especially when I learned of a lady in another village who took her baby to school with her so she could nurse. But I got over it and hired a girl from the village to watch Anne until I got off work. John always had something to do and most of the time it was hunting. I didn't complain too much as he did supply us with ptarmigan later on.

On Friday there was a knock at the door. An elderly Eskimo man was there. In broken English he asked if John might go on a fishing trip with some of the villagers as this would be the last one before school started and winter settled in. Of course John was elated. After thinking it over I decided that if we were to survive out here we should get involved in village life, at least a little. We packed him up with items we were told he would need. With John gone for the weekend I had time to think as I worked. *No television, no radio, no way out of the village except a charter plane! What had I gotten us into? So far the kids loved having other kids around to play with, but we were certainly isolated from the rest of the world.*

On Sunday a storm blew in. John and the fishermen hadn't returned from their trip, so I tried to find out about the missing group. I was told that no one would be able to come down the Kuskokwim or Knak to get home. They would have to go inland across the lakes and slews or camp out until the storm abated. By nightfall I was frantic. There were few people I could talk to because most adults in the village spoke Yupik, not English. That's when I met Barbara and David. Barbara was a white teacher who had married David years earlier and was now a permanent resident. It was a relief to meet someone who spoke English fluently and knew what was going on. (Later I was to learn that David was our cook at the grade school and Barbara taught in the state high school.) They were very supportive of my concerns and explained that this was just part of village life. They assured me the fishing party would probably arrive later that night.

Sure enough they did. John was hyped up and excited as he told of his great adventure. They had been out on the river when the storm hit so had moved inland to the lakes, which they would paddle across. When they came to the marshy areas everyone bailed out, took hold of the boat and pushed or carried it over the soggy ground to the next lake. That was how they made their way home. Of course John was soaked from head to foot and inside out even with his rain gear, but as far as he was concerned that was just an added bonus to his thrilling adventure.

When he came up for air I asked, "Did you bring any fish home?"

"Fish!" was his reply. "I just had the greatest expedition of my life and all you can think of is fish?"

During that same storm a barge filled with heating oil was headed for Bethel but pulled into Tuntutuliak to get out of the worst of the weather. The captain got panicky about going on into Bethel after the storm. He was afraid he might become caught in ice. If that happened, his barge could be frozen in all winter and the movement of the ice might possibly break up the boat. Therefore, he asked the villagers if they would purchase his oil. As it was getting late in the season the natives worried that no other barge would be able to make it to the village so quickly rolled their barrels down to the edge of the river.

The barge waiting on the Knak River to unload the oil

Each fifty-gallon barrel was marked with the owner's name. The barrels were filled and the barge headed south. Most of the barrels sat along the river's edge to await the first snowfall. At that time the townspeople could use their sno-gos and sleds to haul the oil to their homes as it was needed. Before the snowfall, wheelbarrows had to be used to transport the barrels. Not such an easy task! (Snow machines were called sno-gos in Tuntutuliak and snow machines in Napakiak.)

Ready or not school opened the next day. I would teach fourth and fifth grades and ESL to third graders. Each of my students would require a separate IEP (Individual Education Plan) because of the language. They didn't begin speaking English in school until third grade and then only one class period a day. This was a concern for me as Anne was in second grade. There was a third grade girl who spoke English. The principal moved her into my class but wouldn't let me bring my daughter into an English speaking class. I was frustrated because Anne was spending her time coloring instead of getting her second grade education. Basically she lost a year of schooling, but I felt the experiences of living in the village would be valuable and lasting.

Life soon settled into a pattern. I would teach until three in the afternoon and then send Anne to her babysitter until I finished about five. After that I'd go to our apartment where many times I'd find John and his friends playing cards or cooking. His friend Jessie loved to cook, and I was never quite sure what new foods I'd find when I arrived home. I especially loved the fry bread he made.

One day I opened our door to a low rumble. When I couldn't see the end of my living room for the sea of kids I loudly announced, "EVERYONE OUT!" I decided it was time to set down some rules as I counted thirty-five students filing out.

Once everyone was gone we had a family meeting. It was decided that from then on there would be a limit of three friends for each of the kids. That would assure no more than eight kids in the house at one time.

I also realized that some of the kids came mainly to use our toilet because at home they had "honey buckets." The children didn't realize that constant use made it necessary to continually clean the water, which was a nuisance. (We learned quickly about "honey buckets" the next year when we had to use one for several months. A "honey bucket" is a bucket that is used in place of a toilet. They draw flies, but not because of the sweet smell.)

Working for the government meant paper work! School began on August 24th and by September 3rd I had to have a years worth of math planned for my students. To do this required much overtime. When I wasn't working in my room I was working on schoolwork in the apartment. At one of our staff meetings I was amused when a Native teacher suggested that he turn in his yearly lesson plans with, "I will follow the book," written across the page. I loved that!

Not long after school started I was invited to a "throw party." This was a celebration of a child's first "catch." When a child went hunting and brought back their first donation of food for the family there was a party. It didn't matter whether it was a bird or larger game because each addition to the food supply was important. This was a tradition that had been carried on for years.

Naturally I went, but being a guest I decided it would be in my best interest to just observe. It didn't take long to realize the older women took this event very seriously. I was intrigued to find that the "throw party" consisted of the mother of the hunter sitting on the roof of her home with a large variety of goods she had purchased or made. There was everything from a washtub, to candy, to material and towels. The women of the village gathered below and as the mother threw items down, everyone grabbed to get whatever they could. During this party a young boy slipped in and snitched some gum. Immediately, the older women ostracized him verbally until he gave up his gum to one of them. Only girls and women were involved in the "throw party". It didn't matter whether a boy or girl had made the "catch."

The next day we were invited to a birthday party at the home of Anne's sitter. Both Anne and I attended. We entered the house and sat on a couch in the entry waiting our turn to eat. People ate in the order of their arrival. When our turn came we were seated at the table and served on paper plates. Wanting to be helpful when we finished, I gathered up our plates and put them in the huge garbage container in the corner of the kitchen.

From the shocked looks on everyone's face I knew something was definitely wrong and asked, "What happened?"

The hostess pointed to the container. All she said was, "Water!" Wow! Did I make a booboo!

Since I had running water in my apartment and at the school, I hadn't realized that without running water huge plastic garbage cans were used as the water supply. The villagers hauled their water from the lakes to the houses. They stored the fresh water in one large trashcan and the used water in another. Unfortunately, I had just put the garbage into the container of fresh water.

I was mortified but the hostess was great...after the initial shock. She smiled and graciously said, "The water was almost gone anyway."

Anne and I made a quick exit and I decided I'd best consult Barbara before taking part in any more village functions, or at least pay closer attention to what others did while there.

Curious now about the water supply for the village I decided to go to the Hunter's apartment and ask why we were the only ones with running water. Also, I wanted to know what happened to *our* waste as we lived on permafrost and with year-round frozen ground there would be no way to put pipes underground or pump anything into the ground. I had already figured out that living on permafrost accounted for the use of "honey buckets" instead of outhouses. Although there had been outhouses built for the school, they were not being used. Permafrost also accounted for the millions of mosquitoes on the tundra. As the tundra thawed out a foot or two in warm weather it provided a perfect breeding ground. The story goes that if you got lost or stranded on the tundra you would die from mosquito bites before you starved.

When I asked Hunter my questions he explained as we walked to the recycling room. "There is one well that supplies the school and school personnel. This was dug at government expense. Once the water is used, whether in the kitchens or bathrooms, it goes to the recycling room located in the southeast corner of the school. There it is run through several machines, tested weekly, then run out through a pipe into the large lake beside the school."

When Hunter told me that lake was also the major source of water for the village all I could think was, *YUK!* But he further explained, "I know it is hard to believe but when tested it is found that the water going out from the pipe AFTER being recycled is the purest in the village. That is BEFORE it empties into the lake and becomes subject to the multitude of germs in the lake water."

My thought then was: *The villagers might be better off collecting their water from the school's recycled waste before it went into the lake!*

Each night when I finished work at the school, Anne would be close by waiting for me. One night she was nowhere to be found. Since the source of communication throughout the village was the CB radio, I called on the school's CB to Anne's babysitter to see if she was there. I was told she wasn't, but before I could leave the office, a call came in from Upper Village. "They are playing at the high school," an unknown voice said. "I'll send her home as soon as they come back." It was then I decided to never say anything on the CB I didn't want everyone to hear. Each household kept their CB on at all times to keep up on what was happening in the village.

A few weeks after John's fishing trip the same elderly gentleman who had invited him knocked on our door. He had some dried fish. He said it was for us because of John's help on the trip. I thanked him and we ate the fish even though I had some reservations after having seen those fly-covered fish drying on the housetops. Actually it was delicious, especially since we had very little meat in our diet. It also helped when I found that many villagers actually dried their fish inside away from the flies.

On the first of September there was a knock on the door. As usual I looked out the window to see who it was. The only entrance to our apartment was through the school, but there was a window close to the school entrance so you could see who was on the steps and hear the knock. An old lady was standing on the porch. When she saw me through the window she yelled out, "Selling!" I soon learned that meant someone needed money and was trying to sell you one of their beautiful handmade items. The word "selling" was one English word that everyone knew! This lady was selling seal skin slippers. As much as I hated the thought of killing a seal to make the slippers, I knew that the only source of income for many of the villagers was to make and sell these items. I bought a pair and never regretted the purchase as they were so comfortable and soft I literally wore out the seams within a couple years.

Ironically, the next day I was looking out the window and saw several hunters returning with their first seal catch. It was interesting to see them wheel the blubber around in a wheelbarrow to each home. It seems the first blubber of the year was shared with every family in the village. I was offered my share, but as I didn't know what to do with it I politely declined. The Yupik Eskimos are very polite and considerate people. Even though I wasn't totally trusted, being a foreigner in their land, they treated me with respect.

I had brought enough dried food to last the winter, but it was the type of food that could be packed and shipped. I decided to check out Cooperation Store for some variety. It didn't take long to figure out I would only shop there when necessary. String beans were $1.25 per can, eggs $1.70 per dozen, flour $12.50 for twenty-five pounds, meat $6.00 per pound and Raisin Bran was $3.45 for a very small box. Meat was available only occasionally, while pop was almost always available. The store could hardly keep it in stock even though they ordered large quantities.

Being the entrepreneur that he was, John figured with so much pop being sold he could go to the dump, collect, smash and package the empty cans, then send them to Oregon. When we went home for the summer he would sell them. Actually he did send several boxes of cans home, but as with his other ventures it probably cost me more than he made.

To relax I enjoyed walking along the river or sitting quietly on the bank. The Knak River was a tributary of the Kuskokwim. We were close enough to the ocean that high tides would sometimes cause the Knak to overflow. On this particular afternoon the river had raised enough to cause several of the boats tied along its edge to partially fill with water. Two boys, about eight or nine, were walking along and noticed what had happened. They went from boat to boat dumping out the water and checking the moorings. It was fascinating to see how everyone in the village, even the young, worked together.

One of the interesting things I noticed when school started was the words the youngsters had acquired and included in their vocabulary. If they didn't like something they would say, "That's bum!" They didn't use the past tense. They would say, "Did go," "Did see," or "Did run." Instead of reading a book they would "watch the book". One little boy, when asked a question with a negative response, would answer, "Noooo," which sounded like a stretched out moo. I always thought that was cute. And everything was "maybe." You rarely got a straight answer.

After living in the area a couple of years I began to think that life there ran on "ifs" and "maybes." An example: "If the tide, or plane, came in, maybe someone would go to Bethel." Life was surely much slower and definitely more uncertain.

On September 7, 1980, John brought home his first ptarmigan. We had fresh meat! After that, and thanks to his persistence, we ate ptarmigan regularly. A ptarmigan is about the size of a pheasant and the meat is similar. I broiled the meat and then dipped it in melted butter. It was delicious!

We had been in Tuntutuliak only a short time when Anne got her first earache. In her younger years she had required tubes in her ears two times and over the next three years would continually battle earaches and strep throat. The clinic had a wonderful nurse aid named Cathy who got to know us quite well before the year was up. She was excellent at diagnosing Anne's problems and getting her on the correct medication. The best part was services were free to anyone in the village. We became well acquainted.

(I was very sad to learn a few years later that Cathy drowned on a trip home from Bethel. Considering the fact that rivers and lakes surrounded the village, it was amazing how few villagers could swim.)

We had barely been in our apartment a month when I left John in charge of draining, cleaning and filling the recyclable toilet before he left for school. About 11:00 a.m. the maintenance man came to my classroom to tell me there was water dripping from under our apartment. I knew immediately what had happened and rushed home to shut off the toilet water. John had drained and cleaned the toilet, then left it to fill. He had forgotten to turn off the water before going to school. Water had filled the bathroom and was about an inch deep in each bedroom. Needless to say, I was devastated.

As soon as school was out the kids and I moved everything out of the bedrooms and began scooping up water. A short while later a group of village kids showed up to help, which was greatly appreciated. Once the standing water was up, I handed out towels and everyone would stomp them onto the carpet, wring them out in buckets, and repeat the procedure. After a couple hours of this we had the worst of the water out. Every night we would repeat this procedure. It was over a week before everything had dried out completely and we could again sleep in the bedrooms we had abandoned. We had moved everything around in the living and dining room area and put the beds out there. It was nice to have the house back in order.

John thought he could add fish to our diet if only I would purchase materials for him to make a fish trap. I was hesitant. As much as I enjoyed the ptarmigan I was sure they were the most expensive meat I'd ever eaten because of the boxes of shells I was continually purchasing. I finally agreed to the materials and John worked diligently for some time getting help from many of his friends. Finally the trap was completed. I waited in anticipation for fish to be added to our menu, but it was not to be. One thing after another happened to his trap and finally he gave up on it. (Later, after tasting the bottom fish he was trying to catch, I wasn't too sorry he hadn't been more successful.)

Another time John went hunting with some friends and came home with a muskrat. He was ecstatic as someone showed him how to skin it. He was sure he could make money if he had a board to stretch the skin on. Our neighbor had used the side of his house to stretch his, but we couldn't do that on school property so we rounded up a board. He was able to sell his skin but unfortunately didn't get enough for it to make it worth the money it had cost me.

About this time John began taking steam baths with his friends. He enjoyed this type of bathing, but one day, after getting permission to take a steam, he came home early. When I asked him why he said, "Everything was going great until the girls showed up. I didn't think you would approve of group steams." He was right about that! We were told later that it was common practice for families to steam together although most of the time it was either just men or just women. Also we were told that it was quite fun for the natives to get a gussak (white person) into the steam and then make it hotter and hotter to see how much they could stand.

The end of that first September, Anne's class went on a field trip to Bethel. There they visited the fire station, police station, and most exciting of all, got to stop for hamburgers at the closest thing to a McDonalds that Bethel had to offer.

They had gone by boat. Anne wasn't used to the wind and cold of a boat ride so her teacher, David, put her down in the hold. She was excited as this was her first boat ride, but she was so cold when she got home it took several hours to warm her up. Of all the exciting things they had done though, all she could talk about was "the hamburger!" She had grown up with McDonalds and greatly missed our frequent trips.

Our school was kept running by our maintenance man and head of the school board, James. He reminded me of my Uncle Archie because there wasn't anything either of them couldn't do or at least figure out what to do. Three big generators that looked like the insides of an old Packard we used to own, and about as old, were used to produce our school's electricity. It was James' responsibility to keep them going as well as making sure our water supply was safe—this was in addition to anything and everything else around the school that continually needed repair. He also built the storage shelves and whatever else the school needed.

James owned his own plane. In the winter he used the river as a runway and storage for the plane. It was fascinating to see each wing tied down to a sno-go in order to keep it from being blown away.

James's plane tied down with snow machines

Towards the end of September James knocked on the door and said, "I'm flying to Bethel. I wondered if you'd like me to bring back some fresh vegetables and meat for you and the kids?"

Naturally I replied, "Sure."

That night we had steak and salad. What a treat! Unfortunately that one meal cleaned out my grocery budget for the month. After that I decided I'd best be careful about letting someone else do my shopping, even though it was very thoughtful of James to get supplies for us. Working for the federal government was definitely NOT a way to get ahead.

September 28, 1980, it snowed. Although I had brought the clothes listed I decided it was now time to get Anne some even warmer clothes. I began looking in the catalogs as buying clothes in the village was not an option. There just weren't any.

On the 29th word spread around school that John had shot at his friend Peter. Of course the village officials immediately started an investigation and it wasn't until after school that everything finally got straightened out. Peter emphatically informed everyone that someone had made the story up. He and John had been together and nothing had happened. I guess there is always something for which to be thankful.

By the sixth of October the ground was frozen. By the 13th the lake was almost completely frozen and by the 15th it had begun snowing and snowed steadily for two days. On the 28th the chill factor was -13° and the temperature was +9°. It was then that James said, "This winter when the temperature gets up to 0 you will think it's warm." I just laughed.

That day John thought it would be fun to try to break up the ice on the edge of the lake. Immediately several of the older villagers became upset and told him to stop. Eskimos believed that breaking up of the ice would cause a warm winter.

By October 31, the kids were ice-skating on the village lakes. Winter had arrived!

For Halloween the kids divided into two large groups. One half went to one side of the village. The other half went to the other side of the village. Each group crowded into a home where treats were handed out. They did this from house to house. Then they changed sides of the village. While in each home there was a contest to guess every child's name. If the adults couldn't guess a child's name that person got a prize as well as their candy. Since she wasn't as well known in the village, Anne came home with a huge bag of treats. According to her she had a blast!

John decided to spend his Halloween with Ed's family in Kwigillingok. Ed was a teacher in the state high school and his wife taught in Kwig so he traveled there many weekends to spend time with his family. Once the snow was deep enough he could ride his snow machine between the two villages. That was fine as long as the trail was marked and he didn't get caught in a snowstorm.

That October was not a great month for Anne or me as we were sick most of the time. Anne had sore throats and ear infections while I had sore throats. When I finally recuperated the first of November, I couldn't believe how good I felt.

Living in the village you had to be very self-sufficient. One of the girls asked if I could give a permanent. I told her that I could as I'd been giving perms to my mom and sisters for years. She asked me to perm her hair, which I did. It looked nice and she was delighted but giving perms is time consuming and not one of my favorite things to do. Personally, I hoped that this didn't catch on. Most of the girls wore their hair long and straight and fortunately that was the only perm I was asked to give to the girls.

There had been talk since I arrived about the BIA school going state. Government officials were supposed to come to the village and have a meeting to explain the possible changes. Time after time they didn't arrive when planned. Finally, after several months, a meeting was actually held to discuss the state taking over the BIA grade school, as it was already running the high school.

The meeting was interesting. The questions focused on concerns that the children would continue to get free meals and free school supplies instead of quality education. During the meeting an elderly woman sat in a chair for a bit, then sat on the floor for a while, and finally got up and walked out. Evidently the meeting had gone too long for her. It helped me understand the inability of my students to sit for extended periods of time.

I had taken my photography equipment with me. It was relaxing and fun to take and develop the rolls of film that showed village life. At first I was hesitant to take too many pictures of the people, as I wasn't sure of their reactions. I was afraid my shooting pictures of their activities would offend them. But as the year progressed, I did get some great pictures.

The dry, cold and windy weather made it miserable when I had recess duty outside. Someone suggested I have fur sewn onto the edge of my hood. It would cut the wind and keep some of the cold away from my face. I thought it sounded like a good idea and took my hood to a lady in the village. She sewed about six inches of wolf fur onto the front of it. I couldn't believe how much it helped keep my face from freezing.

At one of our school meetings David (the second grade teacher) asked, "Do we get extra pay depending on whether or not the school board likes us?" Another point he made was, "My students aren't trained to go to the bathroom when told to do so. They know when they have to go!" In order to keep to a routine in the classroom we had been encouraged to have the children use the restrooms during recess, but obviously this hadn't gone over well with everyone.

By the first of November I succumbed to John's pressure and bought a snow machine. He was sure this would allow him to bring in more ptarmigan, as that had become one of our major meat sources. If I'd have known all the trouble he would have keeping it running I probably would have said no—but he sure did have fun, and it certainly kept him busy trying to keep it running.

It wasn't until later I found out what a dealer John was. The man had been trying to sell the machine for $500, but old wheeler, dealer John said, "If you sell it to me I'll give you $600." I think he missed the point that you're supposed to deal down, not up! Then of course he only needed a few more things: shells at $13.00 a box, an ax to chop ice, traps, an extra belt for the machine, plugs, and oil. All told it was another $100. The good thing was, someone offered to buy the machine from us at the end of the year if we didn't return.

We had barely gotten to enjoy feeling well when Anne got sick again. Her temperature went up to 104° and I couldn't get it down. I got so worried I contacted the mail plane office and asked about going into Bethel. They said a plane would be in shortly, so I bundled Anne up and John took us to the airstrip on the sno-go. After sitting there for almost an hour her temperature went down, but no plane showed up. About that time James arrived and said he needed to take his plane to Bethel. He would take Anne and me with him if I would pay for the gas. Of course I agreed, as we still hadn't heard from the mail plane.

Thanks to James I got Anne to the hospital. By then she had pneumonia, infected ears, and other viruses. We spent the night at the Kuskokwim Inn as the hospital wanted to check her again in the morning to see if she was well enough to return to the village. That night was a nightmare. The walls were thin and the inn was filled with drunks. I was so scared I couldn't sleep. I finally pushed the dresser and chairs up against the door. Feeling somewhat safer I was able to at least sleep for a couple hours.

Then next day the doctor decided Anne could recuperate at home. We caught a mail plane back to Tuntutuliak where John was waiting with the sno-go. As quickly as possible we got Anne home and into bed. She slept a lot and seemed to be getting better until four days later. She began throwing up her medicine and her temperature spiked again.

I left John with Anne while I went to use the phone. After getting cut off six times while trying to explain Anne's condition to the doctor, I finally gave up and went home. The doctor called back to the clinic on the CB. He explained that the temperature went along with pneumonia. Cathy came to the house to give us the message. She checked Anne and said her chest was better, although her ears and throat were still bad.

Finally, after almost two weeks, Anne was able to attend school for half a day. Having her ill so far from doctors and a hospital was indeed frightening. The doctor thought that her constant ear problems might have something to do with the pressure and weather changes in Alaska in addition to her already damaged ears.

I was very fortunate to have a wonderful person to help with Anne while she was sick. Lucy came over each morning to stay with her while I was at school. Anne loved her, and Lucy was always kind and patient. One day when she came to babysit she brought us some fish strips, which were delicious.

My problem was the cost. It seemed I spent a fortune to keep Anne in babysitters, as she was sick so much. Even when she was well I paid sitters after school.

When Anne wasn't feeling well and was confined she would get cranky as an old bear. Peter and Jesse loved to come and play games with her because she was a challenge, but they also loved to argue with her. I finally told them they argued worse than John and Anne. The bad part was Anne had learned enough Yupik by now that she could hold her own in an argument. I wasn't always sure that her choice of words was appropriate for an eight year old.

One day I came home to find John and three of his friends in the bathroom trying out my curling iron. It was pretty funny to see the results. Of course Charlie, the oldest, was careful to smash his hair down flat before he left. He said he didn't want to look like a girl!

A store in Bethel had supplied our school with pumpkins for Halloween, so I had each student in my class write a thank-you. Then I took a picture of them and their finished Jack-O-Lanterns. I developed the picture and sent it with the thank-you letters to the store. My picture was printed in the Tundra Times. That was exciting for both the kids and me.

The school had ordered a movie for Halloween and kept it for several weeks. While Anne was ill we watched it over and over. By the fourth time I had gotten pretty tired of the *Maltese Falcon*, but it kept Anne down and quiet for at least a while. She also completed a Distar Reading Workbook just for fun and something to do.

In late November we were invited to another birthday party. This time I was much more careful and didn't try to be helpful. That party turned out fine.

John went hunting almost daily. On one of his excursions onto the tundra the sno-go quit and he had to walk home. Of course he was completely bummed out. The next day Hunter said he would take John out to try and get it started. They weren't successful. A couple days later, after listening to him whine continually, I was thankful when Carl's dad showed up at our door. He asked, "John, have you gotten your machine started?"

"No," John told him.

Carl's dad said, "Come on, John, let's go get it!" Sure enough, he took John out and fixed the machine for him. I was continually amazed at how self-sufficient and ingenuous the villagers were.

That night Carl stayed with John. They got up EARLY the next morning to go hunting. I never had to worry when John was by himself, as he didn't go very far away so if (and when) the machine quit he could safely walk home. It was when he went with someone else that they seemed to get a little braver. I was never sure what might happen then.

In November our postman had a snow machine accident and was sent to the hospital in Anchorage. When his wife went to visit him we were left with no one to take care of the mail. Then on the 21st of November everything seemed to shut down. The weather wouldn't permit the mail plane to land and the phone lost service. There was no outside communication, except the CB. The isolation now seemed overwhelming.

On the 23rd President Reagan closed down all government agencies to save money so we had an unexpected day off. Now that was something I couldn't complain about. Since Anne wasn't going to school I didn't have to pay a baby sitter. It had also been my day to have playground duty. I sure didn't mind missing playground duty! I stayed home, took care of two sick kids, and baked rolls.

On the 28th John and his friend Porky went hunting. They got seven ptarmigan between them and only used fourteen shells. That was pretty good because the day before John had gotten one ptarmigan with fifteen shells. As much as we enjoyed the ptarmigan I wasn't sure I could continue to afford his hunting and told him so when I found out it had taken him fifteen shells for one bird. John was upset because I wasn't sufficiently excited over his ptarmigan and said, "You complain too much about the cost of shells and gas when I'm bringing home meat for us to eat."

I explained, "Since I'm the one making, and forking over the dough to purchase these items, I think I should have a little say as to how often they are replenished! You're welcome to try and find a job to pay for your own hunting supplies."

The problem with that was there weren't jobs available in the village and I did enjoy the meat from the birds. But it seemed that every cent I made was going for gas, shells, juice and babysitters! (The doctor had said to give Anne plenty of juice to drink because of her constant infections.)

I cooked a turkey dinner for Thanksgiving. Jesse and Peter J. had come over to play games with Anne and when John and Porky got back from hunting they all joined us for dinner. I baked my bread for dinner as well as for the dressing. It was a nice change from dried food and ptarmigan. I made a banana cream pie out of dried bananas, which wasn't too bad.

The boys and Anne played games and argued until about 8:00 p.m. when Willie and Mary Moon showed up with dried salmon and agutak. (Agutak is Eskimo ice cream. It is berries whipped into Crisco and sugar. They used seal blubber in the past.) We sort of visited. I say "sort of" because Mary loved to visit but spoke only Yupik. Willie actually spoke English very well although in all the times he had come to the school I had never heard him speak anything but Yupik. He never even let on he knew English.

Saturday morning I baked bread for the Moons. That afternoon it warmed up, started raining and got sloppy wet outside. Then it snowed and thawed so everything was one big muddy mess. The lake ice had melted about two inches, but when it was frozen so deep two inches didn't really hurt much except to add to the dreadful mess.

On Monday, November 30, a terrific storm hit. It lasted three days but didn't close the school. Not all the kids came, but school went on. We went to the Sattler's for supper that night. Ward Sattler was a high school teacher whose daughter I taught part of the day because she spoke primarily English. Mary was almost the same age as Anne. It annoyed me that Sharon made an exception of Mary since she spoke English but wouldn't allow Anne to be in an English speaking class—mine! Liz Ann, Ward's wife, was an excellent cook and great company. I enjoyed visiting with her.

Our sno-go was broken—again—so when it was time for us to leave Ward drove us home in the high school's all-terrain vehicle since weather had become so nasty. It had been nice not to have to cook for once. Out there if you wanted to eat, you cooked! There was no such thing as a restaurant.

By the next day the visibility was so bad that many Upper Village kids didn't make it to school. When the wind died down there were three-foot drifts in some places and bare spots in others. The kids who made it to school though, loved it. They built snow forts and had snow ball fights at recess. It took a lot to slow them down. The way they dressed made me cringe, but they didn't seem to get cold. It was somewhere between -20° and -30° degrees below zero and Charlie didn't even have a hat on. Peter put his hands on Charlie's ears and said, "Charlie has no freeze here!"

And then there were my kids. They started the morning donning their long johns and then their clothes. John had coveralls and a heavy coat with a sealskin hat to cover his head. Anne dressed in a similar manner with snow pants and a heavy coat with a hood. They both had pullover hats that covered their faces.

By the 4th of December, Anne was sick again. Her ears were draining and John had a cold so I took them both to the clinic. I thought, *How wonderful it will be when we are all healthy—even if it is for only a short time.*

That same day a plane with five of our village kids on their way to a basketball game broke down and made a nosedive landing out on the tundra. Fortunately no one was hurt!

Henry, our third grade teacher, was gone all that week and I had his students as well as mine. At times like this I wished I were a bit more like him. He was an outstanding teacher—always patient, never raised his voice or got mad and always had control of his kids. If a child disobeyed he would quietly remind them of their responsibilities. With all of his kids, but not his patience, I was tired and grouchy by the end of the week. I felt like sitting down and crying, but instead I lay down for a while and then made orange rolls. (Love those orange rolls!!!)

On the 8th of December another blizzard hit. It wasn't quite as bad as the last one but when it was over the day was clear, crisp and beautiful with a gorgeous sunset. My classroom was situated so in winter the sun rose through one window about 10:30 a.m. and set about 2:30 p.m. through the one beside it. That winter I had spectacular views of both sunrises and sunsets. If I happened to be busy some student would usually remind me to check out the window. What an uplifting experience!

One day John decided to cook supper for David, Barbara and Ed. I helped him a little, but he did most of the work. It turned out great, but we started chatting after the meal and I realized how careful one had to be. With only six non-natives in the village, gossip could certainly cause hurt feelings.

John's sno-go had been broken for some time. When James volunteered to fix it for $5.00 I was thrilled and immediately agreed. The weather finally warmed up enough to snow.

The closer it got to Christmas the more depressed I became. The kids at school were hyper. It was difficult calling home as the phone was out a good share of the time. When the mail was able to make it in we got packages from home. I thought they would cheer me up, but instead they had the opposite effect. I guess I was just homesick!

On the 17th I was literally exhausted when school got out for the weekend. When I got home Anne and two friends had been playing and the house was a shambles. John had invited Ed to supper; then taken off leaving me to cook. Oh, how I hated to cook some days! This day certainly didn't add anything positive to my disposition.

That night Mark, one of my students, got his leg caught in a snow machine track. It was badly mangled and he needed to go to the hospital, but it was dangerous to bring a plane in at night. The villagers had to line their snow machines up around the airstrip and shine their lights on the runway so the plane could land. After some debate it was decided to wait until morning to airlift Mark into Bethel. Before morning the ice fog settled in, which kept him in the village. Even the mail planes couldn't move for three days. Everything was covered with ice and the fog was so thick you couldn't see for more than a few feet. Cathy, the nurse, did the best she could for Mark, but there wasn't much she could do for the constant pain. During those three days though, he never once complained. Sure made my complaints seem minuscule!

On Monday the 20th the weather finally broke and Mark was flown to Bethel. In order to get more specialized care and therapy after his leg was repaired, he was flown to Anchorage. It was several months before he returned home. Two years later I saw him again and was amazed that he had completely recovered from his ordeal.

The day Mark was flown out to Bethel six or seven mail planes landed. It seemed that mail just kept coming and coming. James was in Bethel when the fog lifted and said it looked like a fleet of jet fighters as the planes took off one right after another.

The Mt. Edgecomb kids had been stuck in Bethel and were afraid they might not get home for Christmas. Before the high school was built the older kids went to Mt. Edgecomb High School near Juneau for their education. Some still left although most now stayed in the village for their high school years.

The 20th was also my birthday and my best present was knowing that Mark was on his way to the hospital. John, Jesse and Peter make me a birthday cake and invited David, Barbara and the Hunters to share it with us.

Actually, the cake we ate was the second one they had baked. I found the first cake in a cupboard the next day. It tasted horrible, was flat and hard. When I asked John about it he said he wasn't sure what had happened. We went over the recipe and when it came to, "1 tablespoon of baking soda," we figured he had mistakenly put in one CUP. He didn't make that mistake again and we put that cake right where it belonged— the garbage!

December 23 was the last day of school before Christmas. We had a party and several students saved their presents to take home and open on Christmas Day.

For a Christmas tree John went out on the tundra and found a gangly little evergreen, as there were very few trees on the tundra to choose from. Once on a visit to Bethel I had noticed a sign that said, "Bethel National Forest," with one lone tree behind it. (I got a big kick out of that!)

On Christmas Eve, the 24th we had our Christmas. The kids were excited because the gifts from relatives, as well as the gifts I ordered, had arrived. We were very lucky. With the bad weather and the mail getting piled up in Bethel some folks didn't get their Christmas orders.

Anne was into Strawberry Shortcake and received several "shortcake" items so she was happy. Lucy made her a Cuspuc (a top that had long sleeves and a hood for keeping mosquitoes away) and for John she knit a hat that was very popular in the village at that time. He loved it. She gave me some warm gloves and since my hands always seemed to be freezing, I appreciated them. I made my orange rolls and gave them out to the generous villagers.

That night we went to candlelight services at the Moravian Church. It was packed. The kids loved it because they gave out candy afterwards. I saw that Mary Moon sat on the floor. She was a very unique person.

We had a turkey dinner on Christmas Day and invited the Hunters to share it with us. Hunter started talking about various people in the village and knowing how fast gossip spread I didn't want to get involved, so I gaily sang one line of "Tis the Season to be Jolly!" I guess he got the hint because that ended the gossip.

After they left we had a quiet, relaxing day. I took some of my homemade bread over to the Moons and wrote a letter home asking mom to send me stamps. I explained to her that I mailed two packages, but two days later when I went to the post office the boxes were still there. When I asked about them the postal lady explained that they didn't have any stamps with which to mail them. They had to wait until Bethel sent stamps, which they had to pay for ahead of time. Even when the stamps were paid for Bethel could be slow sending them out.

The next day Anne was sick again. John went out to work on his sno-go and managed to get it running—again, but in the process lost my two large crescent wrenches, which didn't make me very happy.

The village water supply had been frozen for some time. The lakes were frozen so deep it was impossible to break through the ice for the water. Ice became the water supply. Villagers used sno-gos and sleds to haul it. The older boys hauled ice for the elderly. Just another example of how everyone contributed to the welfare of the village.

Hauling ice for the local water supply

On the 28th the Corporation Warehouse burned right in the middle of three homes. Fortunately there was no wind that night. Though there was a firehouse it did no good, as there was no village water supply. Mostly the people watched although some threw snow on the fire while others rushed to the school for fire extinguishers and water. We were the only water supply in the village. Fortunately the other houses didn't catch fire.

Later I was reprimanded for sharing our fire extinguishers. Sharon said we should have saved them in case the fire spread to the school. I hadn't thought much about it at the time. She was handing them out, also.

School was back in session between Christmas and New Years. That way we could get out in early May so families could move down river to fish camp for the fishing season. On Monday many of the students didn't bother to come to school, so on Tuesday when some boys decided to go hunting John asked to go with them. There were so many kids absent I let him go. I didn't think he would miss that much. Hunter and Sharon were livid with me because they said I should have been setting an example by keeping my kids in school and encouraging the others to come during the week. The next day five of my twelve students were absent. I don't think John being in school or out had any affect on the other kids in the village. School never was a priority and hunting always took precedence. In fact, so many kids were absent I had the class study for a while and I worked on my objectives. I decided to go for a two in my evaluation.

On Thursday there was only a half-day of school. That afternoon there was a wedding to which I was invited. The ceremony was similar to one we might attend at home.

That night I tried calling my parents, but there was no answer. I was distraught, as it was difficult to get to the phone and actually find it working.

On January 1, 1981, I went to an Eskimo New Year's Party. I walked up to the high school gym where the party was held. It was fascinating to see over thirty sno-gos lined up in front of the school. What a sight!

Everyone sat on the floor and we played games. For fun and laughs some Eskimo volunteers did the "gussak walk." (A gussak is a white person.)

The mail planes came in again on the second of January. Plane after plane landed. What a day! Along with our mail, John got two ptarmigan and once again we had meat. He spent the next several days home sick.

The one good thing about cold weather was that the sunrises and sunsets were more gorgeous than ever.

On Thursday, January 7, the wind chill reached -120°. At that temperature your skin could freeze in a matter of seconds if exposed; at least that's what I was told. The swirling winds and snow were so dense I couldn't see the house ten feet from my living room window. By noon the winds had died down and an announcement was made over the CB. School would be held that afternoon. Many students were unable to attend as huge drifts had piled up around their doors. It took the rest of the day for villagers to dig each other out.

On January 8th, school was dismissed at noon for the beginning of Slavaaq, which is the Russian Orthodox Christmas celebration. I visited the Russian Orthodox Church and then went to Slavaaq for a while. Slavaaq lasts for several days. Everyone crowded into a home where food was served, a lighted star was spun and people sang songs. After a couple hours they moved to the next house. This went on day and night until each home had been visited.

I wanted to take part in the activities. I filled my plate with several different food items as I entered the one and only home I visited. I then moved to the back room. There was standing room only throughout the house. I picked up what I thought was a piece of meat from my plate. When I held it up two eye sockets stared at me. I was so astonished I gasped. Someone near me said, "Mink head. Good!"

Carefully I put it back on my plate and picked a tiny piece of meat from the bone to taste. I smiled back with an, "Oh, yes," and then proceeded to eat items that I was sure I could identify. After visiting one house I was ready to go home.

During Slavaaq when the kids did come to school they were so tired we didn't accomplish much. John loved Slavaaq and I let him attend—but not for all night. As usual Anne was sick so spent most of her time at home.

On January 10th Ed sent us some hamburger and ice cream from Bethel. What a great treat! That same day the toilet quit and it was two and a half days before James could get it fixed. During that time we had to use the gross school toilets, which was still better than a honey bucket!

Right after that the weather warmed up enough to snow, then the winds came. It snowed and blew constantly for three days leaving huge drifts everywhere.

By the 15th Anne was really sick. I wasn't able to contact the doctor, so I decided to take her to Bethel. We spent the day waiting for either airplanes or doctors. When we finally got to see a doctor he told us to go home and wait ten days. If she got better fine, if not they would send her to the hospital in Anchorage for tests. Fortunately she got better.

I got a letter from Cindy asking me to call home. The phone wasn't open. Then a blizzard hit so it was several days before I could make the call. Of course I worried needlessly. They hadn't heard from us for a while and were just wondering if everything was all right.

Parent conferences were interesting. About half the parents actually came, but since some didn't speak English it made for rather difficult conferences. I was tired after conferences and when I got home I found the kids had made a disaster of the house. It wasn't my idea of a perfect day.

The night of the 21st John was sleeping in the living room, when I heard him yell. I came running out of my bedroom. "What's the matter?" I asked anxiously.

"Someone just stuck his head in the door!" he yelled.

I got the gun and checked out the hall, but didn't see anyone. We locked the door but couldn't sleep. The next day John showed me how easy it was to open our front door from the outside even when it was locked. That night we put a tie on the door so it couldn't be opened at night.

When I told Hunter what had happened he said, "You could get into big trouble for having a gun on government property—the school. You can have it in the apartment but not the school."

That was ridiculous because we had to go through the school whenever we went to our apartment. I informed him, "NO ONE will come into my apartment at night, government or no government, and I will use my gun if necessary!"

I slept with the gun nearby for some time, but no visitors appeared again. We never did figure out who had tried to come in.

The end of January John rode his sno-go to Bethel with Ed and some other villagers. He had a blast. He even saw a couple of the dog sleds come in from the Kuskokwim 300 dog sled race, although he "forgot" to take a picture. I'm not sure what they did, but this little trip cost me sixty dollars and John a frostbitten finger.

Pickups on frozen Knak River
Rising tides push ice up into ridges along the edges of the river

I woke up Monday morning, January 25th, with a dreadful case of the flu. I ached all over. It was one of the worst cases I'd ever had. John had it too, but not quite so bad. Surprisingly, Anne was actually feeling better. Her medicine was finally working! By Wednesday I was feeling well enough to go back to school. I also finished my evaluation with Sharon. Afterward, she began lecturing me, mostly concerning John.

When we first arrived in the village, Hunter suggested he could be something of a "support system" for John. That didn't last long though, because John was not the best or easiest student. He quickly got involved with the kids and adults in the community and didn't need Hunter. John's interests were hunting, fishing and "hanging out" with his friends. He spent time playing cards and cooking when he was not out on the tundra. I'm not sure what annoyed Hunter most, but it finally got to the point that no matter what John or I did he was on us. Sometimes he had Sharon reprimand us. And when I messed up a disk on the computer...he really became irate.

As the year progressed I became more grouchy and depressed as I was continually being harassed by Sharon and suffering one sickness after another. The one thing that cheered me up was the cards and letters from home. My sister Mary could cheer anyone with her cute cards and letters. Aunt Theresa also wrote faithfully and always sent little surprises during every holiday and sometimes in between. She was a wonderful cook, and boy did I love to open her packages!

No matter how bad things got between the gusaaks I thought we should support each other, as we were the outsiders. So, when at the end of January I was invited to go for a sleigh ride with the Hunters, I went. It was peaceful and quiet on the tundra. The white stillness surrounded you and for a moment you felt a oneness with Nature. We rode out to where the plane had crashed. After seeing the wreckage I wondered how our kids had survived.

As a variance to our diet, I spent time trying to figure out how to grow sprouts. After many failed attempts, I was finally successful and even showed Barbara how to grow them. My first sprout/nut sandwich was scrumptious.

By the first of February things were going from bad to worse with Hunter. Someone got into the school. Of course I got blamed for leaving the doors open. Never mind that the locks on the end doors didn't work and anyone could just walk in. Hunter decided to put locks on all the doors, including the kitchen, so that no one, specifically me, could get in.

I decided that each night I would take a walk through the school and check things so when we went to bed at least I would know everything had been locked up. Hunter didn't like me wandering through the school and called a meeting of the board to discuss the problem. All I could think of was, *What the hell! Things can't get much worse!* Boy was I wrong.

I never heard what happened at the meeting but nothing was done. The federal government supplied the food for the kitchen and every one in the village knew the Hunters used whatever they wanted from the supplies. His rational was that they fed visitors to the village so were entitled to use whatever they needed. Because of the difficulty in transporting necessities to the village, the government sent out larger quantities but less frequently.

My disgust was that there was so much waste. Sometimes they would bring in an entire box of dried fruit that had become moldy from sitting so long out in the little store houses—a couple of them being the old out-houses for the school. When my dryer quit, James brought in a new one that had been stored for several years but found it had rusted out. He brought in another one. It didn't work either. He gave up and fixed my old one. It ran fine.

Much of John's time now was spent repairing his sno-go. He would ask around until he got the information he needed, then go to work. More than once I came home to a mess of parts and tools in the living room. Several times I even got into the act and the day I got the bearings out for him, I was rather proud of myself.

On February 6th the weather warmed up above zero and James' prediction was accurate. It did feel warm. But what a mess! Water was everywhere! I went to Corporation Store to buy the kids new boots so they could walk around.

On Monday morning, February 8th, Hunter and Sharon zapped me again. Nothing about my teaching was correct. My bulletin boards, which I'd spent hours on, weren't good enough. My lesson plans, which did NOT say, "I'll follow the book," weren't good enough. John was a problem, and on and on they went. By then I had begun to realize there was a definite problem here, and I was sure it had nothing to do with my teaching.

About this time I was told in no uncertain terms by Hunter, "Sharon and I ran off last year's teachers and we can certainly do it again."

Right then and there I determined they weren't going to run me off. I had signed an agreement to stay the year and knew if I didn't stay I would have to pay back the cost of the tickets to get there, which had been over $2000.

Why they disliked me so much I never did figure out... unless it was because I had become friends with several people in the village. The interesting thing was that one day I couldn't do anything right and a few days later they would invite me on a sno-go ride or bring over a pizza.

I pretty much made up my mind that this would be my only year in Tuntutuliak. Also, I learned that if I went to work for the state of Alaska I could almost double my salary.

On that particular day when I went home from school I was feeling discouraged. Then I found both John and Anne gone. I remembered John had asked to take Anne with him to check his traps—another expensive venture he had gotten into. They should have been back before I got home. By now it was dark and I was terrified something had happened.

Quickly, I went to Barbara and David's and asked for help. David got up, put on his outdoor clothes and headed for the tundra. He met them on their way back. The sno-go had gotten stuck in a drift and John hadn't been able to get it out. He put Anne on the hood of the machine while it was running to keep her warm, as she hadn't dressed warm enough for this late in the evening. He kept trying to get the machine out of the drift. Fortunately a young man named Brian had come along, pulled them out and followed them home to be sure they made it. He didn't think the machine sounded like it was running to well…as usual!

I was pretty hysterical by the time they got back and all I could think of was, *Thank God for Barbara, David and Brian!* While David helped John fix his sno-go, I took Anne home and got her into a hot bath. What a day!

It wasn't until later I learned what had really happened that day. Evidently John let Anne drive the sno-go. She accidentally pushed the handle too hard and the machine started spinning around in circles. He yelled to her, "Let go! Let go!" She let go and the machine slid off the ice into a snowdrift. Anne thought it was pretty exciting. I thought it was pretty frightening.

We had been without mail for several days when a plane finally made it in. It's amazing how you begin to listen, not just with your ears, but with your entire being, for those planes. They were the lifelines to the outside world. Even now on a still summer day when I hear the drone of a plane's engine overhead I have this strange feeling that I'm connected. And I STILL love that sound!

John's sno-go broke down again. It was becoming a joke. It seemed his machine was down more than it was running.

The village finally voted on whether to go state the next year. We were told it would be a while before the results were announced. There was lots of talk and speculation about what might happen. Actually it was several months before it was decided Tuntutuliak would remain BIA for one more year.

When John caught his first rabbit we added that to our menu. He spent a lot of time trying to stretch and dry the rabbit skin in order to sell it. But, as with many of his other ventures, it didn't work and the skin was worthless.

On Valentine's Day I cooked a big dinner for the kids and their friends. Then I began packing boxes of things we could do without. I wanted everything sent home by the last day of school. It felt good to be on the downhill side of the year and know I wouldn't have to work with the Hunters again. It surprised me that they continued to make an effort to be friendly at times.

The principal for the high school served several schools, so I walked up to ask Ward when she would be in the village. Since she was coming out the following day I returned to the high school the next afternoon to meet and talk with her about the possibility of working for the state. She gave me the paperwork to fill out but told me she didn't have an opening in her schools for the next year, although she had a friend named Don who might have. She asked me to fly to Bethel and meet with him. She mentioned that lasting the year in Tuntutuliak would be in my favor when applying to work for the state.

By the middle of February everyone was restless. The long, dark, cold days began to greatly influence emotions and attitudes. For a change, and something to look forward to, the children and I decided to spend the weekend in Kwig with Ed and his family. Kwigillingok was further down the Kuskokwim right on the Arctic Ocean. We chartered a plane and at the appointed time went to the runway, but as usual had to wait in the cold for over an hour before it finally made an appearance.

Arriving at Lanay's house in Kwig

When we arrived at our destination Lanay had a turkey dinner waiting for us. We had a great weekend eating and visiting. While there, I met a young man named Doug who also worked for the BIA. Naturally we discussed the possibilities of working for the state. We agreed that it would be a much more profitable venture than working for the BIA.

(Later that year I heard a story about Doug and an experience he supposedly had on a long snow machine trip he had taken with a friend. It seems that after several hours of riding across the tundra he realized he had to go to the bathroom...seriously.

When traveling in that extreme cold, you always wore several layers of clothing. Many times it was too cold to stop, undress and do your thing. It would be very difficult, and probably impossible, to remove those necessary clothes, quickly do your thing, and redress fast enough to avoid getting frostbite on the exposed parts.

So...they stopped in a nearby village and went to the home of a friend of Doug's traveling partner. Inside the home the friend explained Doug's predicament and the native immediately, graciously offered his facilities. He pointed to a covered bucket near where the rest of the family sat watching TV. It turned out to be their honey bucket. Now Doug had three choices: 1) Go in his pants—yuck, what a horrible trip home. 2) Go outside and freeze those exposed parts. 3) Use the honey bucket with the entire family sitting practically next to it. Of course, number three was his only real choice so he proceeded to complete his business while everyone else went about theirs as if nothing unusual was occurring.)

We came home from Kwig Sunday on the Sea Air mail plane. Flying Sea Air was much cheaper than the charter. The plane was crowded when we left Kwigillingok, so I held Anne until we landed at Kong and someone deplaned. I didn't mind because of the savings.

Hunter had his sno-go and sled at the airstrip when we landed at Tuntutuliak. He volunteered to give us a ride home. Once we were in the sled he tore off down the river at tremendous speed, the sled swaying alarmingly. I was sitting on my knees holding Anne in front of me. As we neared the school Hunter turned sharply and swung up over the riverbank. A boat had frozen into the bank. As the sled skidded sideways we crashed. The edge of the boat tore into my side of the sled smashing my legs against the back of the sled. I screamed and grabbed Anne tighter. Evidently Hunter felt the pull because he turned, realizing what had happened.

I was in terrible pain and my legs felt numb. Hunter jumped off his machine, took Anne out of my arms, and lifted me from the sled like I was a rag doll. He carried me to the apartment. It took several days for my legs to recover. Hunter seemed extremely upset over the accident. I wondered if he was driving like that to show off.

That night when Anne was changing clothes I noticed a mark on her ribcage. It turned out to be my handprint. I must have grabbed and held onto her so tightly I left my handprint. I was aghast thinking I might have broken a rib.

After having been accused of leaving the school doors open, I still made my "rounds" each night before going to bed. I would carefully check every outside door and walk through the rooms just to make sure no one was there. One night as I was checking the end doors I heard a noise coming from Hunter's classroom. Noiselessly I checked the door, but it was locked. I started back toward my apartment; then decided I'd best find out what made the noise. I didn't want Hunter mad again if someone was messing around in his room.

There was a second door to his room from a hallway off my classroom. I quietly tiptoed through my classroom and through the narrow hall, slowly opening the door to his room. I couldn't immediately see anything but the lights were on and I was sure I had heard a noise. My concern was that kids might be hiding in there after hearing me approach, so I took several steps into the room to better see who was there. You can imagine how horrified I was to see Hunter on the floor on top of one of our native aides. I quietly and quickly retreated. Since he was so "involved" I wasn't sure he had seen me and was terrified of what he might do if he had.

Hunter had been giving me a bad time over just about everything, even threatening to "run me off". I decided it would be best to cover myself with some sort of protection. After thinking about what would be the best way, I finally decided to write a long letter to my sister. I explained the situation and requested she put it in my bank lock box in Oregon. I told her if anything were to happen to me she should give it to the police. I had included in the letter everything I had seen that night; dates, time, and etc. plus all the harassment I had received from Hunter and Sharon. I made sure I included when and where they had threatened to "run me off."

For some time I double-checked our door each night, put chairs in front of it and slept with the gun close to my bed.

Evidently Hunter was unaware of my discovery as nothing was said and his harassment got worse, especially towards John. It got so bad I wasn't sure I could finish out the year, but I didn't have the money to quit and pay back the BIA. Besides, I wasn't a quitter and was determined Hunter would not "run me off."

One day when things were especially rough, I called my parents to tell them what was happening. They suggested I send John to stay with them. At least then Hunter couldn't harass him to get even with me. I agreed and told them I would see what arrangements I could make. By then I was afraid Hunter might actually do something to harm John.

Not too long before this, David had become fed up with all that was going on at school. So, tired of all the hassles and accusations, he quit and went to work for Sea Air. It was to him and Barbara I talked that weekend about sending John out to Anchorage via Sea Air ASAP. I didn't want Hunter to know what was going on so David said he would quietly make the arrangements. He knew Ed planned to go to Anchorage. He planned to arrange for John to fly with him. Ed could then put him on a plane to Portland where my dad would pick him up. I thought his plan sounded like a good idea and asked David to please make it happen.

Convincing John was a whole other ballgame, but one I managed to pull off. In our family counsel, I impressed the importance of silence on the subject to both John and Anne. Fortunately I didn't have to go into detail as to why I had made such a sudden decision. Both children were quite aware of the harassment being inflicted upon us.

On Monday morning I walked into Sharon's office and casually told her, "I am withdrawing John from school as he no longer lives in the village."

Sharon was so surprised that her mouth literally dropped open but she managed a, "Why?" I didn't choose to enlighten her. I turned and walked out of the office.

That ended some of my problems with the Hunters. Even though I never said a word, the village people had not been blind to what was going on. Being very family oriented, they were quite irate that Hunter had broken up our family.

I had no idea what impact my actions might have, but I knew that I *could* make it through the rest of the year. The next time I went Corporation Store to get meat they handed me the key to the freezer instead of having a youngster from the village open it for me. It was a nice feeling knowing their attitude towards me had changed.

After John left I needed something to cheer me up and decided to order a little black and white television. I wanted to see if I could get some news from the outside world. After going through the Sears Catalog, I ordered a portable one that could easily be sent. Then began the wait.

As the weather began to warm up the first of March, the Northern Lights were out in all their splendor. The Eskimos, according to the kids, believed that the Northern Lights were powerful and years earlier had taken up a villager who had "called them down." One night a student was showing us how you "called them down" by whistling, after which he quickly ran home so they wouldn't get him.

Without John it was pretty quiet around the apartment. Jesse still came occasionally to cook and play cards with Anne, but it wasn't the same. I went to the high school and took a couple of photography classes, tried to get organized at school, and also prepared to move out of the apartment.

On March 13, a gussak couple, Al and Diane, moved into David and Barbara's old house. I decided to get acquainted. Al had been hired to put in a washateria for the village and Diane traveled with her husband.

I decided to invite David, Barbara, Diane and Al to supper one weekend. We all had a great time getting acquainted. Soon, Diane and I had become great friends.

I spent the first couple of weeks in March filling out the application material for LKSD, the state school system. From March 13th through the 22nd, we got mail once and on the 22nd only new mail came through; no old mail. Finally on the 23rd we got the back mail. Boy is mail important when you are isolated.

With the back mail came my television. I was eager to try it out but found there really was very little reception as a snowy screen greeted me most of the time. Oh well, at least I could occasionally get the news.

Anne's birthday was the end of March and Julia, one of her baby sitters, stayed the night. The next morning they went around the village collecting the girls Anne's age before returning to our apartment to decorate the birthday cake. They used the leftover frosting to squirt into each other's mouths.

Fortunately the mail had come in with her presents before her actual birthday and then, after much anticipation, Anne opened her gifts.

Usually I didn't let so many children come in at the same time, but everything went great. They had a great time and played for over two hours before dinner was ready.

Anne had planned the dinner, which consisted of turkey, jell-o, potato chips and cake. Everyone helped set the table. They ate, then played for several more hours. Some of the adults decided to play volleyball at the high school, so after most of the kids left Anne invited Agnes to go to the gym with us. When we returned she spent the night. They got scared in the night, which meant I got very little sleep!

One of the things I got Anne for her birthday was a pair of mukluks. Mukluks are high boots made of sealskin. They were so cute and comfortable she wore them all weekend. After seeing how much she liked hers, I later bought myself a pair.

One of the things I observed was that the natives, especially the elderly, seemed to shuffle as they walked. I found out quickly, after purchasing my own mukluks, that when walking on icy ground, shuffling was one way to avoid slipping and falling.

On the 31st of March the Title I people came to evaluate our school. When it came my turn I couldn't have been happier. They complimented me on my record keeping as well as my teaching. After all of the hassles I had gone through with Hunter and Sharon I was pleased to have it confirmed that I actually was doing a good job. Hunter's only reaction was a little "dig", but what could he say? After all, I had been told how well I was doing by the professionals. That certainly overrode any of his remarks. (Carolyn was one of the ladies who came to evaluate our school. I later taught sixth grade with her in the Matanuska-Susitna Borough School District.)

That same day Ed made ice cream, brought some down and invited the Hunters over without mentioning it to me. Ed didn't know anything about what I had seen, but I was unmistakably nervous around Hunter. Nothing was ever said about me walking into his room that night, so I was never did know whether he had actually seen me.

On April 1st, I caught Sea Air to Bethel, rented a car and stayed the night at the LKSD dorm. I splurged and bought a juicy hamburger and a real milkshake. They tasted especially delicious, as it had been a long time since I had eaten restaurant food. Maybe my system wasn't used to that kind of food any more because I suffered all night with diarrhea and a stomachache.

The next day I personally took my application papers to the LKSD office where I visited with the same lady whom I had met when we arrived that fall. She remembered me (not many BIA teachers show up there in the middle of the night) and seemed pleased I had decided to work for the state.

Next, I went to the BIA office where I turned in my resignation. When I met with Cal, I was surprised he knew much of what had been happening in Tuntutuliak. He said, "I'm sorry about your stay out there, but appreciate your lasting the year. There are some other openings we have, and you can have your choice if you'd like."

I looked over the positions and saw that one was at Little Diomede, the closest island to Russia. I declined that offer as I had heard the story of someone flying into the school there and it taking a month before she could get off the island because of the bad weather.

No, my decision had been made—I wanted somewhere close to a good medical facility because of Anne. Also, I had decided I would prefer working for LKSD because of the money.

Before I left Bethel I bought a perm for Diane. The next day I gave Diane the perm in the morning and in the afternoon packed more boxes in preparation for mailing home.

As I already mentioned, while in Bethel I had suffered a rough night of nausea and diarrhea but thought it was something I had eaten. Even though I felt much better the next day, the vague feeling of nausea had not completely gone away—it was just there lurking in the background. By Sunday morning I was extremely ill with flu-like symptoms. I slept from Sunday afternoon until almost noon Monday. I felt better by then so went to school. I never was quite sure whether I had gotten some bad food or picked up a flu bug.

After school was over for the day, I went to the government building to call home. I was disappointed I couldn't get through to my parents. While I was in the booth, the building was closed, locked and vacated. Evidently no one thought to check the phone booth. What a bummer! I had to use the CB to call for help as the door was locked from the outside. The next day I tried calling home again and was successful both in reaching my family and in getting out of the building before they locked up!

The Friday before Easter we had only a half-day of school. That morning, after the kids had decorated eggs, we hid them outside in the snow. The students didn't mind at all—the eggs were easier to see that way.

Diane came over that afternoon to do her washing. While the clothes washed and dried, we played cards and cooked soup for supper. Before leaving Oregon I had purchased much of our food from a health food store. Since Diane was also into nutritious eating it was fun to fix new healthy meals. It was also more fun to cook with someone else.

A blizzard hit on Saturday and we stayed home. Jesse came over to help Anne bake cookies for Easter. Sunday noon we went to the high school gym for Easter dinner. It was potluck.

What fun tasting so many different and delicious foods. I admit though, I checked out the meat to make sure there were no eye sockets! After the potluck we stopped and had tea with Liz Ann. That night Diane and Al came over for supper. All in all Easter turned out to be a very positive experience.

Shortly after Easter the CTBS testing began. Our raises for the next year were dependent on the outcome of those tests. Even though I didn't plan to be teaching for the BIA, I still felt a need for my students to do well.

After finishing the reading portion, I was very discouraged. My students had been in Yupik speaking classes until third grade and then in only one English speaking class a day. It was not until the fourth grade that their English education began full time, yet my fourth graders were expected to take the same tests as all other fourth graders! And...any salary increase would depend on the outcome of those same tests.

Once the students started the language arts, math, social studies, and science tests, they did much better and in the end I would have gotten a raise. They especially did well in math and I was very proud of the tremendous effort put out by the children.

By April 15th Anne was sick again! Fortunately, this time it only lasted four days. By then, as soon as she became sick, Cathy would put her on medication.

I continued to send boxes home almost daily as I slowly cleaned out the apartment. Some of John's old friends stopped by one day and hauled all my trash to the dump. I appreciated how thoughtful the kids could be. I think they missed the days when John was there. Something was always going on at our apartment then.

On April 19th I told Sharon I was quitting and on the 21st, after she finished my final evaluation, I was pleasantly surprised that I scored as high as I did. I always wondered if my quitting and sending John home influenced her evaluation.

Diane and I decided to have a yard sale with items we didn't need and didn't want to mail out. Al was almost done with his part of the washateria so they would be moving. We put up signs and set out our goodies. I was pleased and surprised with the results, because at first no one seemed to know what a yard sale was. Once word spread and people got the idea of what a yard sale was, we sold everything. We figured that yard sale was another first. It was -10° that day!

After Diane and Al had packed and shipped their things they stayed at the apartment for the last few days. We played cards for hours. It was disheartening knowing how much I would miss Diane when she left. Since she arrived we had spent most of our off-work hours together. The good thing was she helped the time pass quickly those last months!

Graduation was the third of May. That was also the day that the birds began returning to nest on the tundra. The kids were WILD! They "shot" everything that flew by the classroom window and there was literally flock after flock of various birds. Each time a flock arrived all the boys jumped out of their seats, ran to the window and shot their imaginary guns. Obviously we didn't accomplish much educationally that day!

Don Young, Alaska's Congressman spoke at graduation. It was an impressive ceremony.

On the 7th of May I flew into Bethel again. On the way the pilot asked if anyone was smoking. There were six passengers on the plane including Cathy, the nurse from Tuntutuliak. We all assured him we were not smoking. He radioed Bethel to tell them he smelled smoke. Bethel suggested he land at Napakiak and they would send a plane out to pick us up. He responded that he was sure he could make it on into Bethel. I looked back at Cathy and thought, *Well, if we crash, at least we'll have a nurse with us.* We made it into Bethel and never heard what was wrong with the plane. But I was sure of one thing. I didn't want to return to Tuntutuliak on ***that*** plane!

The next morning in Bethel I met with Don. We discussed different job possibilities. He had accepted the principal position at Napakiak and there were several openings expected. He said he would like to have me teach for him and sounded quite positive about the possibility of a job for the next year. But, he couldn't make a final decision until all of the resignations and transfers were in and that would be later in the summer. I would just have to go home and wait!

I spent Mother's Day working in the classroom until about 3:00 p.m. I kept Anne with me. Afterward David picked us up on his sno-go. We went to the high school to work on photography. We enjoyed steak and salad at David and Barbara's that evening while watching the movie, "Every Which Way But Loose." That was Mother's Day, 1981.

On May 11th it snowed and snowed. It snowed again the next day. I was convinced Mother Nature didn't intend to let us out of there with good weather. I just hoped the planes could fly. If the planes didn't fly you didn't travel!

The last few days of school meant cleaning out my classroom, preparing report cards for the students, and packing and shipping the last of my household items. The last day of school was the 21st of May, and I wasn't planning to stay a moment longer than I had to. I arranged for a charter plane to pick Anne and me up and fly us to Bethel as soon as school was over. From there we flew to Anchorage.

As happens so often in Alaska, we arrived late in Anchorage, missing our connecting flight, and couldn't get out until the next day. We went to a hotel where I found they wouldn't take my check. I scrounged through my belongings and finally came up with enough money for the room. They promised a free shuttle would return us to the airport in the morning in time to catch our plane. I had only a couple dollars left so decided we'd have breakfast on the plane the next morning. In those days almost every trip included a meal. It was that experience that made me decide I would never again travel without a credit card. (As soon as I arrived home I did get one.)

I had decided we would travel through southeast Alaska and stop at my aunt and uncles in Petersburg before going on to Oregon. When we arrived my aunt took over. She fed us, took me to her bank so I could cash a check and then suggested nicely that we visit a local beauty saloon to have my hair styled. (I hadn't had anything done to it since I'd left the year before.) I decided I couldn't argue with her on that one!

Since there were several openings for teachers at a village on an island near Petersburg, Alaska, my aunt agreed to fly out with me so I could apply. That was some flight! We boarded a small plane for the trip. We had to fly down a channel between two islands with mountains on each side. As we moved down the narrow passage the plane would suddenly DROP in altitude, rise again and DROP once more! My stomach was doing flip-flops but when I looked back at my aunt I noticed she seemed to be calmly reading a book—at least a lot of staring if not a lot of page turning. Later I asked her how she had remained so calm and she answered, "I could have had the book upside down for all I got out of the story." I thought it was interesting that there was a nurse on this flight, also. It made me think of my earlier flight that month to Bethel when the pilot had smelled smoke.

We finally arrived in Kake, but by that time I wasn't sure I was interested in any positions they might have. Even so, I filled out the paperwork and visited with the lady in charge. She informed me that there were only two ways to and from the island...charter flight or the ferry. There also wasn't much of a town, just a small village much like the one we had left.

My aunt and I decided to take the ferry back to Petersburg. After six or so hours of rolling back and forth over the waves as the ferry *slowly* proceeded on its way, I was sure this was NOT a situation I wanted to be in and dropped the application in the trash as we left the ferry.

By the time Anne and I started home, she had a cold again. As the plane lifted off the airstrip, her ears began to hurt. She was in such pain I called the stewardess to see if she had any ideas how to relieve the pain. Very kindly she got two hot towels and two paper cups. She put a hot towel in each cup and had Anne put one over each ear. By doing this it relieved the pressure enough so she wasn't quite so uncomfortable. Flying down the chain of islands to Seattle, the plane had to land and take off several times. Each time we used the cups and towels to help ease Anne through the take-offs and landings. Finally we arrived in Portland where we were met by Dad and John. It was nice to see John and have my family back together again.

It didn't take long after I arrived home to find out things had not gone well with John. He had continually gotten into trouble at school and caused Mom and Dad considerable trials. I felt bad but knew if I had walked out I would certainly have had a more difficult time getting a job other than BIA.

YEAR TWO

There was nothing for me to do but enjoy being with my family in Oregon, soaking up the warmth we had missed for so many months, and wait to hear from LKSD. I felt I would get a positive call for a job, but until I did uncertainty often kept me a little on edge.

The call from Don finally came. I was offered one of the jobs in the village of Napakiak, which was where I had hoped to go. Almost immediately I started repacking the things the children and I already had and making lists of additional things I knew we would need to live in a village again. As before I had to pack and send everything by mail in apple boxes, but this time I had a better understanding of what I would need. I also knew there was a store in Napakiak that was much larger than the ones in Tuntutuliak.

The previous year I had been pretty careful with my money and even though I had to pay for our flight home, I still had enough left to cover the cost of our move back to Alaska. LKSD didn't pay for our flight to Napakiak, but the salary was so much better it would take only one month's paycheck to cover expenses.

This time our trip was uneventful and we arrived in Bethel for a three-day stay on August 17, 1981 to a pleasant surprise. Both Ed and Lanay had gotten jobs working for LKSD and would be in Napakiak this year. Now I could eagerly look forward to a fun year having at least one couple I knew. Both Anne and John were excited also, because Ed and Lanay had three kids that were about their same ages.

For three days we were put up in a CROWDED dorm in Bethel, which we shared with Lanay and her kids. There were two beds in our ONE room and seven people. Ed slept downstairs in his sleeping bag and the kids slept on the floor. We had some informational meetings to attend during the days. Finally, on Thursday evening Shi-Ming Liaw, who had just been hired by Don, Ed, Lanay and I chartered two planes to get all our kids, bags, and us to Napakiak. We were met by the school's pickup. We quickly loaded our luggage and ourselves in the back and were driven the one-quarter mile to the school. (There was only about one mile of road in the entire village for the pickup to travel on.)

Arriving in a Napakiak The slew (to the left) flows into the Kuskokwim(top).

Upon our arrival we were told our house was not quite finished. It was missing some minor things like water, hear, lights and sewer. Everyone was assigned to share housing, as there were seven family groups and only four houses available. Our house was scheduled to be completed shortly...maybe. "Maybe" is probably one of the most misused words in everyone's vocabulary as we had learned at Tuntutuliak. It meant any time they actually got it done.

The children and I moved in with Don, our principal, until our house became available. The first day of work, one of the couples decided this was not the life for them and packed up and left. Now Don needed two more teachers, including a special education teacher. I asked if he would consider my sister, Sheri. She was not a special education teacher, but would be able to teach the high school physical education classes, home economics and coach girl's basketball.

Don was delighted that he could get someone to cover so many subjects. It was acceptable for him to hire teachers without the correct credentials in order to fill vacant positions if necessary. And since the school year had already started he saw no problems.

It didn't take long for Sheri to decide to accept the job offer. She quickly packed what I told her were the absolutes and arrived a few days later. With four of us now living at Don's it was overcrowded. Sheri and I decided to move as soon as the electricity was hooked up. Fortunately, the electricity was completed within a few days. At last we could move into our new home.

I was glad Sheri was there to share housing costs because the rent was $1200 per month. If I hadn't shared with her I would probably have had to share with someone else. The little house had two bedrooms, a small, narrow living-dining room area, a large pantry, a small kitchen and an entry porch. Eskimo homes had an unheated entry porch so you could get out of the cold and wind to take off your outer layers of clothes before entering the heated part of the house.

It was decided that Anne and I would take one bedroom, Sheri the other and John would set up in the entry porch. We figured by leaving the house door part way open the entry would stay warm enough for him to sleep comfortably—with some extra warm blankets. He was so happy to have privacy he didn't mind at all.

We had heat and electricity when we moved in, but no water. A honey bucket in the furnace room would have to do. The furnace room was off the front entry and with two doors between we hoped it wouldn't smell up the rest of the house. We scrounged up garbage cans and John hauled our water using Ed's sno-go and the school sled. Now we, too, had two garbage cans in our tiny kitchen—one for clean and one for dirty, used, water. The school provided the ability to shower and wash clothes.

Before flying north that year I had purchased a small colored television and a Nintendo with several games. This purchase soon caused problems. These games were popular with the kids and again our house became the village hangout after school. Quickly, Sheri and I had to set down the numbers rule so we could actually get inside after work.

When the school district planned to build the two housing units in the dip behind the school the natives warned them against it. They were right, as usual. The wind swept down into the dip and the houses, which were built on stilts, rocked somewhat like the ferry I had ridden on from Kake! Building the houses on stilts, though, turned out to be a good thing. (The stilts were about four feet high.).

We had only been there a short time before the heavy rains and high tides arrived causing the water in the Kuskokwim to overflow. I laughed when I told people we had water front property. Not only did we feel like we were on a ferry in a storm, we looked like one. We had water in the front, back and under our property.

Evidently this situation had been anticipated as a walkway, also on stilts, had been built between the two houses. We were able to walk down the walkway to the large aboveground sewer pipes, which handled the school water and waste; then walk down the pipe to almost dry ground. With mud boots on we could usually arrive at school fairly dry.

With the flood and winds our electricity went out. We were told it would be fixed right away—maybe. So once again we were cooking and eating at Don's house but sleeping at our own house using flashlights for light. The kid's only complaint was they couldn't play the video games.

Lanay taught first and second grades, I taught third and fourth, Lois taught fifth and sixth, and Ed taught seventh and eighth grades. John was now in the eighth grade. It was nice having Ed teaching him as this eliminated most of the problems of the year before.

Lois's husband and two other teachers taught high school. Sheri taught advanced studies to the English speaking kids in grade school, home economics, high school physical education and girls basketball.

We had only been in Napakiak a couple days when our maintenance man came in with a load of salmon. He said he missed the boat that purchased the fish so his salmon would have to be dumped unless we could use them. He already had what he needed for his family. Don asked what I thought, as he didn't want to freeze them himself. He offered me the use of his freezer if I would be in charge of preparing them. Of course I immediately said I'd take them all.

He brought us fifty-nine, huge, fresh salmon. Don said that it was common practice to freeze the salmon without cleaning them. That sounded great to me as we had so many. I chopped off the heads and tails and together we wrapped them in tinfoil and froze them "as is." Whenever we wanted a salmon steak it was easy to slice off a section, cut out the insides in a circular motion and cook. The salmon meat didn't break down as fast that way and we ate baked salmon, salmon steaks, salmon loaf and even had salmon sandwiches.

The salmon lasted until late in the year when Don's freezer quit. Boy did we have a stinky mess to clean up. Spoiled fish is not the easiest smell to get rid of. It took several days of cleaning in, under and around the freezer before we could walk into his house and NOT smell rotten salmon. But all the effort was worth it. The salmon were absolutely delicious and definitely helped keep our food budget down. As it turned out we lost only four or five of the original fifty-nine fish because we had eaten so many. (Although from the smell you would have thought we lost the entire fifty-nine!)

With my sister Sheri in the village and sharing the house, I decided to volunteer for the new text adoption committee. We met in Bethel once a month at LKSD's expense. It was a nice break and I had no concerns for the children knowing Sheri was there to supervise them while I was gone.

On the first trip I was astonished when my roommate turned out to be a woman named Sue. She and her husband had been teachers in Tuntutuliak the year before I arrived. They were the ones Hunter had bragged he "ran off." We had a lot in common and shared our experiences. I was amazed that we both had similar problems with Hunter and Sharon.

One morning, as we stepped out of our room, we were shocked to meet Sharon coming down the hall but not nearly as shocked as she was. Her mouth dropped open and the look on her face was one I wish I could have captured on camera. She paused, looked at us and asked, "You *KNOW* each other?"

Sue responded, "Oh, yes, we're good friends," which would turn out to be true as we spent the year working on the same committee and later taught together in the Matanuska-Susitna Borough School District in Palmer, Alaska.

Sharon stood there too astonished to say anything. Sue and I walked on to our meeting having thoroughly enjoyed that chance meeting!

After one of my trips I returned home to find John cleaning the bathroom with a toothbrush! I found out he had disobeyed Sheri. I just laughed silently and left him to his task. He would soon learn it was NOT in his best interest to disobey his aunt!

Sheri got involved in village life and was invited to go ice fishing among other activities. The fish they caught were the same bottom fish John had tried to catch in Tuntutuliak. They were rubbery tasting and couldn't compare to the salmon we had stored in the freezer. I wasn't sorry he had been unsuccessful with his fish traps.

Sheri also became the village hairstylist. The girls usually wore their hair long and straight, but once they found Sheri could cut hair, they came to try out a new "do." Before the year was out she had cut every girl's hair in the village between the seventh and twelfth grades except one. Because of her cheerful, willing attitude and her involvement, she was given a beautiful pair of rabbit mittens, which she wore on her trips to Bethel.

Anne was in my class this year. I felt considerably better about her education, but I'm not sure she did. At times she felt singled out because she thought I expected more of her than the other kids, which was true since she could speak English. Fortunately Denny, Ed and Lanay's son, was also in my class and this made it somewhat easier on Anne, as I expected the same from him. Sheri was soon assigned to teach both Anne and Denny in a more advanced class part of the day which helped break up her day.

That year my students had classes in both English and Yupik. Liz was my assistant teacher. She taught the Yupik classes to one grade while I taught English to the other. Then we switched. It was fascinating to watch her teach Yupik, as some of their words are so long they would fill the entire blackboard. For me it was quite a challenge to teach youngsters with such limited English backgrounds.

It was much easier that year for me to obtain supplies, both food and clothing. There was a large store right behind our house and people from other villages, as well as from Bethel, came there to shop. It had many grocery items to purchase as well as a nice clothing section.

Sheri rode into Bethel with Don when he took his sled and snow machine, which was quite frequently. This also provided us with needed supplies. She would hop on the back runners, hold onto the bar and ride into town. I thought it looked like a cold way to ride, but she seemed to enjoy it. She would do our shopping in Bethel. I never needed to worry about the budget because she was even more economical (cheap) then I was.

In Napakiak John found what every young person wants. For the first time in his life he felt he fit in. He spent so much time traveling with Ed in Tunt and Erik in Napakiak that he knew the land, was an above-average hunter and in the bush of Alaska that made you accepted. (As many shells as he had used in Tuntutuliak he certainly should have become a good hunter.) He tells his story in his own words:

> "I realized that I fit in for the first time several months after moving to Napakiak. Amongst some friends one day just out messing around, one of the toughest boys in the village looked at me and said, 'I like you. You're not like a regular gussak.' As compliments go for a youth, he may as well have called me superman. I showed him my thanks and friendship the way any young man would. I laughed and promptly shoved him in the mud."

Sheri loved to decorate which made Thanksgiving special as our house had a festive atmosphere. She was also a great cook and baked two delicious pies to go with our dinner. (And NOT from dried bananas!) Don came over and we ate so much I was miserable for days. (What a different atmosphere than last year!)

I purchased a snow machine shortly after we arrived in Napakiak. It was an adventure to ride to Bethel, which was only twelve river miles away. On a good day we could make it in twenty to twenty-five minutes. One night after school in November five of us decided to make the trip. The river was frozen and well marked so we had a great time going in. When traveling the river one followed a certain trail of flags or markers of some kind. Once the river was frozen the tide came in over the ice. The water at the top froze so when the tide when out, there would be layers of ice with water or air trapped in between. The edges of the river didn't always freeze, especially where slews entered, so it was imperative that you follow the marked trails. It was not uncommon for someone to go out on the ice where it was not safe and fall through. Their body might not be found until spring when the ice melted. We were lucky this first year because the river froze solid and no lives were lost.

On the way home we actually lost the trail, but it was pretty hard to lose the river. Since it was frozen so solid, we were soon back on track and made it home without any further problems.

For Christmas Ed invited his mother to come for a visit. He met her at the airport, caught the taxi and headed for Napakiak. His mother had heard about a river and asked where it was. She was rather disconcerted when she found it was directly under them. What an unusual feeling to actually drive on a river! After our year in Tuntutuliak Anne had told my aunt in Petersburg, "We can walk on water."

My aunt's response had been, "You and JC and the Gang!" Anne didn't get it, but she was still impressed with the fact that we could walk over the lakes and rivers in winter.

We spent Christmas in the village and what a difference from the year before when we had been all alone! With Sheri and Ed and Lanay's family we had a great time. On New Year's Eve we had a big bash with an abundance of food and fun.

During our Christmas break Sheri and I sewed. We had ordered Frostline kits and made vests and other warm items. We even sewed vests for Ed and Don.

Sheri also cut and curled my hair. I wouldn't have to go home this year looking like I had the year before. Since John and Anne had gotten new Atari games and videos they kept busy over the vacation. As always Aunt Theresa sent yummy goodies!

John purchased several traps and set out his trap line in the hopes of getting rich selling various skins. I had been through that last year, so I didn't hold my breath.

For Valentine's Day Theresa was at it again and we all got chocolate goodies. When John wrote to thank her for the candy he told her about joining the wrestling team. He was pretty excited about that.

As coach of the girl's basketball team, Sheri accompanied the girls to their games in the surrounding villages and the only way to get there was to fly. One such game was held on Nunavak Island located in the Arctic Ocean. During the game a storm blew in. As they prepared to leave the wind was whipping around so ferociously it flipped over a plane waiting for another team. That was enough to shake everyone's confidence and Sheri was feeling nauseous by the time they boarded their chartered plane. Unfortunately she wound up sitting in the tail section. With the wind whipping the plane around and her queasy stomach she started heaving. By the time she arrived in Napakiak she was so sick it was almost a week before she fully recovered.

Unfortunately if you want to travel in remote Alaska you have to have faith in your pilots or you will rarely leave the villages. After that flight to Bethel when the pilot had asked if anyone was smoking I remember Cathy commenting, "I would have felt safer flying with Jim. (That's not his real name.) He's crash-landed several times and no one ever got hurt." That comment didn't give me much confidence and I thought, *If he has crashed so many times, I'd just as soon take my chances with someone who hasn't crashed. I don't want to be on his plane when his luck runs out.*

Sheri and I decided we'd invite our sister Cindy up to visit during her spring break in March. She had turned down her chance to teach in the Alaskan Bush and this way we thought she could see what she'd missed, so we bought her a ticket.

Don was out of town and volunteered to loan us his machine to run to Bethel and pick her up. I would ride my machine and Sheri would ride Don's. She would bring Cindy back with her since Don's machine was the larger of the two. We left the kids in the village with Lanay and headed down river. I was sure I could get us to the airport as I'd been in once with Don to pick up some supplies.

We had no trouble getting down the river as it was frozen at least six to eight feet and the trail was well marked. Someone had buried sticks with flags on them all the way to Bethel. Once in Bethel we headed out over the tundra to the airport. It turned out I didn't know the way as well as I thought, and we kept tipping the machines over in the huge snowdrifts.

Finally though, we made it to the airport in a rather roundabout way and went in to await Cindy's arrival. She entered the airport wearing heals, nylons, a suit and a light coat. (It was almost spring in the Portland area.) Immediately we whisked her into the ladies room and in a few minutes had replaced her clothes with John's outdoor gear right down to his long johns, seal skin hat, facemask and goggles.

Anne and Cindy preparing for a snow machine ride

Glancing in the mirror on the way out of the restroom she was astonished. It looked like she had gained ten pounds and you couldn't see an inch of skin. Sheri and I laughed because we dressed like that all the time when traveling.

We quickly headed for our snow machines and explained to her that we would be riding down the river. Naturally Cindy was apprehensive until we explained that the only other options were to wait for a taxi—which could take a day or two and still go down the river- or charter a plane, which would cost about $100 one way. She decided the snow machines would do so we headed back to town by a different route, this time with Sheri leading. We were soon on the river heading to the village. Fortunately it was nice weather, about 20 to 30 degrees above zero, so the trip was quite comfortable. On Saturday we had her on the snow machine again. This time she was in the driver's seat and loved it!

Don arrived home on Sunday and suggested we take Cindy on a tour of the surrounding area. We agreed and headed out. We visited several villages and ended up in Bethel where we ate supper before going on to Napakiak. By the time we arrived home we had put almost 100 miles on our machines. Unfortunately I picked up a 'bug" that would plague me until I arrived back in Oregon for the summer where I was diagnosed and treated for Giardia (beaver fever).

The weather turned cold the week Cindy was visiting and she found out what it was like to travel in extremely cold weather as the wind chill was about −40 degrees when we took her back to the airport. Here, in Cindy's own words, is her rendition of the trip:

> "When the plane landed it was so exceedingly cold I couldn't imagine anywhere as cold as that. As I got off the plane I thought, *This is like the <u>Lion, the Witch and the Wardrobe.</u>* You aren't just going to a different location; you are entering into a different world. I couldn't comprehend not driving on a road. We just got on snow machines and followed the river. I was worried that my sisters knew where we were going

and if the river was solid enough to ride on. I remember thinking how desolate it was with nothing between Bethel and the village to help you locate the trail. My sisters had to teach the next day so suggested I try cross-country skiing, but again the weather was so exceedingly cold that I came home. When we went on our 100-mile excursion I was again struck by the fact that there were no landmarks and I wondered how people got around without getting lost. I also noticed how small the houses and even the villages were and wondered how one kept from being claustrophobic."

I had played baseball during the summer before going to Tuntutuliak. I injured my heel, possibly by stepping on a rock while chasing the ball. Anyway, it had bothered me off and on during the previous year, but now the pain was becoming more constant. I went to several doctors but they couldn't find anything. It was suggested that I might have heel spurs. Donut heel pads could possibly relieve the pressure and whatever was causing the resultant pain to my heel. I purchased the pads and also added little sponges to put under them, but as the year progressed so did my heel problems. The bottom line was, according to the doctors in Bethel, I would just have to live with the pain as long as it didn't get too much worse.

We were scheduled to get out of school on May 5th, which meant there were only eight weeks of school left. This also meant we would have more Saturday school. We had Saturday school every other Saturday during the months of January and February and would continue to have school *every* Saturday through March and April. Saturday school allowed us to get out several weeks early, but it sure made those last six-day weeks long and tedious.

Shortly after Cindy left the weather turned warmer causing the river to start melting. There was so much overflow water on the ice I was chicken to go out on the river. The overflow water could get deep and scary, so we were more or less confined to the village. Both Sheri and I were more than ready to leave for the summer. Running around on the snow machines all winter had spoiled us.

Snowball fights were as popular in Napakiak as in Tuntutuliak and like most children both John and Anne loved to get involved. There was one particular fight in April when Anne tricked John by pretending she was on his side. Then she smashed all his snowballs so the girls on the other side could really blow him away. He was a good sport about it and thought it was both fun and funny.

The school year was finally over. We were all looking forward to seeing family in Oregon. That summer would be a nice change, as I would not be waiting for a call. I had decided to return to Napakiak for another year.

Year Three

My decision to return to Napakiak the next school year made life easier that summer. It was a nice change not to spend the summer waiting for a call, unpacking, repacking and mailing *all* household items to our destination. Knowing what was available, as well as how and where to get food, was a big relief. This allowed me a relaxing summer with my children and family.

Ron had sold our farm, so with some of my share of the money I took John and Anne on a Mexican cruise and then to Disneyland. Boy, did we enjoy the nice warm weather, which was quite a contrast to Alaska.

Though we left most of our belongings in Napakiak, we still had several boxes and bags to carry on our return trip. I even managed to take an exercise bike, as it was difficult to get much exercise during the cold winter months. Each of the children had acquired a kitten, and we had them, and all their paraphernalia, along.

In Bethel I found I needed a rather large charter plane in order to transport our belongings, especially the box containing my exercise bike. We helped the pilot load, and when everything was in John reached over and pulled the sliding door closed. Usually I rode up front beside the pilot, but this time I relented and allowed John to ride in the copilot's seat. That decision may have been a blessing in disguise. I was riding in the seat nearest the sliding door. Shortly after we left Bethel I noticed the sliding door was *slowly sliding open*! I tapped the pilot on the shoulder and motioned to the door. For a moment he appeared to panic. I yelled, "Should I try to close it?"

"NO!" he yelled back. "Stay belted in!"

I carefully reached over, pulled some boxes away from the door and held them so they wouldn't slide back towards the partially open door. Fortunately we were on a short hop, so the pilot slowed down and moved closer the ground. When we landed and deplaned he was rather upset with John, but I calmly suggested that it was *his* job to check out the plane before taking off. There was no real harm done, except maybe to the pilot's nerves. We, and all our belongings, had arrived safely in Napakiak ready to start a new year.

John walked the short distance to the village and asked Don to bring the pickup for us while Anne, the cats, and I waited patiently at the airstrip.

It was nice to arrive with our house set up and ready to go. Since Sheri had decided not to return, there would be some changes. Mainly, I would have to pay the entire $1200 a month rent as well as do all the cooking!

There was a nice addition to our house—a telephone! We actually had a telephone *in* the house! What a convenience! Occasionally we lost service but being so close to Bethel it was usually quite dependable and repairs were done quickly.

The state had decided to remodel our school that year and we were without heat for almost a month. Because of this many students and teachers wound up getting sick. Anne and I both got colds, then strep throat and had to go into Bethel by boat for medicine.

We had a great clinic in the village and of course Anne and I were frequent visitors when we couldn't get to Bethel. By the end of that year the nurse at the clinic decided Anne might be a strep carrier because she had it so frequently. (After we left the villages she rarely got strep again.)

Shortly after arriving in Napakiak John found a new venture...GOLD. We knew there were gold mines upriver from the village. John reasoned that it was probable flakes of gold could have washed downstream. He spent several days wading along the edge of the Kuskokwim. He was excited when he began finding specks of shiny gold-colored rock. He carefully sorted out the flakes, brought them home, cleaned them up and placed them in a jar. After several days he had a nice little collection. I even got interested so decided I'd try to find out if this was actually gold. It was...FOOL'S GOLD!!! The end of another get-rich venture!

The previous year we had gotten by with one snow machine but John wanted a four-wheeler this year. There were times when the wind blew the snow away and you couldn't travel on the river with a snow machine. He was sure a Honda Oddesy four-wheeler with roll bars (like a dune buggy) was the answer. They didn't have any in the village but on a boat trip to Bethel with Eric he found just what he wanted. John made a good argument so I agreed check it out. I was persuaded and bought one.

Eric took John to Bethel in his boat to pick up the machine. On the way back John climbed into the seat and fastened the seat belt. He got so excited pretending to ride his new four-wheeler over what must have been rough terrain he rocked the boat and almost put his new machine at the bottom of the Kuskokwim River.

According to Eric, "I could just picture the boat tipping over and John going into the river, with his seat belt on, so I told him to come and sit with me."

Poor John, he only had his machine for one day when it broke down. I called the dealer but the only way they would do anything was if we brought it back to Bethel. "NOW WHAT!" I was totally disgusted that they weren't more cooperative. I was so irritated I thought I might return it but was told I would lose $600 if I did. When I approached Eric he wasn't too enthused about trying to get the four-wheeler back to Bethel after the last trip. His boat was actually rather small for the job anyway. When Don heard of the problem he suggested checking with the crew that was remodeling our school. I had very few choices so I looked up the crew boss and told him our predicament. He said they took their boat in every few days for supplies and it wouldn't be any problem to transport the machine for us. As their boat was much larger it would also be a safer trip.

Sure enough they took John's machine in on their next trip to Bethel. They left it at the dealers and when it was fixed picked it up and returned it safely to us.

Secretly I wondered if John might have accidentally done something that caused the breakdown. Therefore, I was doubly thankful when the dealer told me it was actually a manufacture's defect that had caused the problem and I wouldn't have to pay for the repairs. We didn't have any more trouble with breakdowns the rest of the year.

John was thrilled, but the machine wasn't all he had anticipated. It was great on the tundra and the trails around the village before the snow fell, but the back tires were large and heavy and after the snows arrived he was continually getting hung up in the snowdrifts. Also, it would break through the river ice if it wasn't thick enough. Eric expressed his concern about John going into the river with his seat belt on, and between the seat belt and roll bars, not being able to get out of the water. I talked with John and kept my fingers crossed.

One of the teachers Don had hired the year before was a lady named Shi-Ming Liaw. She had rented an old Eskimo house in the village with no indoor facilities. Her husband worked in Bethel so she would catch a ride in to see him on weekends with anyone who was going into town.

One native man she had ridden with several times became interested in her and began coming to her house, especially when he had been drinking. She wouldn't let him in, but he would try the door and windows anyway. The situation scared her enough that Don asked me if I would share housing with her.

It didn't take me long to agree. She was delighted to have a warm, new home to live in. I was delighted to share the rent and have another great cook in the house. We had been missing

Sheri's cooking, but it turned out Shi-Ming was also a great cook. We all loved Chinese food, which was her specialty.

Her admirer showed up at our house only one time. When I opened the door there were several shotguns visible directly inside. He never returned and I often wondered if that information wasn't passed on because we were never bothered by anyone in Napakiak.

Shortly after school started John was invited to go on a weeklong moose hunt to which I agreed. They took boats up the Kuskoswim River about two-thirds of the way to Anchorage near the Cook Inlet, then down the Stony River. John got two beaver, a couple of geese and the group got a moose. John saw moose, deer, a brown bear and other smaller game. He had a great time and we got a nice moose roast out of the trip.

This is John's story:

"Being a good shot I was never in short supply of hunting partners and it wasn't long before I was invited on my first major hunting trip—a moose hunt. (My hunting skill was cultured in part by necessity as my mother had supplied me with a single shot shotgun. If you didn't get your prey on the first shot, by the time you reloaded, usually it was gone! I got real good, real fast.) The moose hunt was quite an experience. On our third night out we set up camp in the trees, deep in moose country, along a river. The Eskimo are very superstitious and any unknown noises were said to be ghosts or spirits. At dusk, after a dinner of fish soup and hard crackers, I heard a noise in the trees and wanted to explore. Reluctantly my two buddies agreed to go with me while the adults were trying out the boat and settling in with tea or coffee. Not far into the trees it got a lot darker. We heard movement but couldn't see anything. Their fears were contagious and we were soon all jumpy. A rustling in the trees and what sounded like a scream turned us toward two glowing orbs floating in a tree. My buddy screamed! Four shots rang out followed by a scream that sounded like a woman dying. We all bolted back to camp. The adults were waiting at the tree line with mixed looks of concern and fear on their faces.

"We stayed up late trying to scare one another by outdoing the last story of what it was in the woods and how it would come and get us while sleeping. Sleep did finally come though and I was the first awake at dawn and excited to see just what traces might have been left behind by the animal/monster we had heard and seen the night before. Sticking my head out of the tent, I froze. At the waters edge stood two moose drinking like they hadn't a care in the world. Slowly I pulled back and excitedly shook awake our hunting party, who were at first resistant to my urges until they realized what I was saying. In a flurry of clumsy movements my friend's father stepped part- way out of the tent in his long johns and deftly shot the moose through the lungs. It collapsed with a loud thump in the mud on the bank.

"The animal was HUGE and a small chainsaw was used to cut away each leg. It took both of my buddies and me to drag one leg the twenty feet down the bank to the river. About three and a half hours later the moose was fully dressed and loaded into the boat. The beach looked like a war zone with blood trailing all over and all of us were bloody and muddy from head to toe and dead tired!

"After cleaning up and eating we had time to relax for a while before heading back to the village. As I relaxed, memories of the night before came back and I grabbed one of my buddies and headed back into the woods. The spent shotgun shells were found and we trekked through the underbrush towards the trees where we'd seen the ghostly orbs. On the ground lay a dead screech owl. Realization dawned on me and I slapped my paranoid friend on the back and started laughing. We laughed till tears came; closure to an unknown fear. Sated, I picked up the small majestic bird and sadness overcame me. Now perhaps there was a free spirit lost in the winds of the trees. We buried the little warrior and went home.

"Back at the village the moose was divided among four families. The huge moose, approximately 2000 pounds, provided plenty of meat for all. In addition to a couple geese I had shot on the way back, I was awarded a moose steak that probably weighed at least fifteen pounds. This was a meaty meal for the whole family and an award for being a part of the conquest—just another long weekend in the Alaskan bush."

By the end of October our winter was already settling in. The temperature oscillated between -30° and +30°. The river was jammed with ice and many of the slews and lakes were already frozen. The kids were enjoying skating. There wasn't much snow, but if the cold held we would be able to travel the river in a couple weeks. We were looking forward to that. We had enjoyed running safely to and from Bethel the year before and could hardly wait for the river to freeze again this year.

There is a large permanent fund in Alaska from the years of high oil prices. Each year it is divided among the families that reside there. We might get anywhere from $300 to $1000 a year for *each* individual in the family. Having a large family certainly came in handy during that time of year!

Once our dividend checks arrived the children and I became impatient in our anticipation of a shopping trip to Bethel. John wanted to buy gas for his four-wheeler. In preparation he had scrounged up a fifty-gallon barrel, built a small shed to put it in, and purchased a lock. He was ready! Anne was more interested in new clothes and toys, and I had my own agenda.

Finally the day came. Several villagers were making their first trip to Bethel and had agreed to let six of us follow them in. It took almost an hour to get dressed for the trip. Next we got our machines up and running and went to join the group. It was then we got the news. The natives had decided they weren't sure the river was ready for traffic. One thing we were to learn that day was *always* listen to the natives.

The kids were disappointed, but Eric said he would wait until around noon and let us know if things changed. We returned home and removed our travel clothes to impatiently await the verdict. Around noon Eric said he had decided to go. Don and Ed had already left. If we wanted we could follow him.

We put our traveling clothes back on again preparing to leave. Everything went well, and we arrived in Bethel just in time for John to fill his gas barrel. The station was closing as we pulled in. Eric was carrying a smaller gas container, which he also filled. Then we went to the store. It carried everything from clothes, to toys, to food, to outdoor necessities. There we met Don and Ed. They got into an argument with Eric, so instead of waiting for us they took off for home.

We finished our shopping and headed out. John stopped shortly saying he had to go to the bathroom. He headed for a snowdrift while we waited. Just as he was returning a dog sled approached at tremendous speed. Unfortunately, one of the dogs had gotten loose and its trace line was swinging out from the team. The loose trace line caught Eric's snow machine runner pulling it sideways. Eric and John ran to help the driver stop his team. Those dogs are bred to race and once going they don't want to stop. Finally though, the three men were able to get them calmed enough to unhook the trace from the runner. The runner was bent but Eric figured he could still make it home.

John jumped on his machine not noticing that the sled had tilted. His four-wheeler didn't run well in deep snow so he gunned it to get enough power to start the sled moving. That was all it took! The sled tipped and the full barrel of gas broke the side out. We got the sled righted, rolled the barrel back on and headed out. Our concern now was that the barrel not shift to the broken side.

We hadn't gone far when the ice started cracking under Eric. John's sled was much heavier and Eric feared John's gas barrel would break through the ice taking John with it. He had John disconnect the sled and leave it there, saying they would return later to retrieve it. John had invested quite a bit of money in his barrel of gas and it was with considerable reluctance he unhooked the sled. Once again we headed for home.

Eric decided to have us travel single file with John in the lead, Anne and I in the middle, and him bringing up the rear. That way he could better monitor our travel and not leave one of us behind. John didn't know the way so just followed where the trail led. I had assumed Eric was monitoring our progress, as I didn't know this trail either. But Eric was so concerned about the cracking ice he hadn't noticed we'd missed a turn. Suddenly we rounded a huge drift and there was open water. It was too wide to jump and it didn't look like there was any way around, so Eric decided we'd best turn back and find a more suitable trail.

He decided he should lead this time. Trying to keep up was difficult because John's four-wheeler kept getting stuck in snowdrifts. Time after time I would jump off my machine, run up to give him a boost or help him lift it out of the snow, jump back on my machine and then we'd try to catch up to Eric.

By now it was getting late and I was getting tired and scared. We stopped to look over the situation. I suggested going back to Bethel and trying to get home the next morning, but Eric was determined to continue on. He said if we didn't find the trail soon, though, we'd go back to Bethel as I had suggested.

We had only gone a short distance when we met two young men from our village. They explained to Eric how to get to the river. Once we reached the river, they said, we could make it home if we stayed toward the center. We followed their directions and finally came to the river, but then were faced with another problem. There was a narrow strip of open water that had to be crossed in order to reach the solid ice of the river.

Eric thought we could jump it. He said he'd go first and if he made it we could follow. He jumped okay but as he landed, his bent runner twisted worse. Now he was more concerned then ever about making it to the village, but he quickly turned his attention to John. John revved up his four-wheeler and made it over, but as he landed his back wheels broke through the ice. Quickly Eric yanked him off the quad and pulled him to thicker ice...and safety.

Now it was my turn and truthfully, after watching both Eric and John, I was scared. I had Anne in front of me and was worried about getting her wet. She could have hypothermia before we got home if I miscalculated. I looked the banks over carefully. I couldn't jump where John had because his machine was in the way. I located a small rise that hopefully would provide enough height to land us farther out onto the solid ice.

I gunned the motor, took off and prepared for the lift. That went okay, but as I hit the ice the runners twisted sideways and the machine flipped on its side sending Anne and me sliding down the ice. Fortunately we weren't injured, probably because of the thick layers of clothing we were wearing which acted as excellent padding. After my initial shocked reaction, and realizing neither of us was injured, I quickly got up and checked out the snow machine. It was okay so we prepared to move on.

Eric wanted John to leave his machine. He wasn't sure we could get it out without going into the water ourselves. I had heard stories about machines being left in the ice. They would freeze in and when the ice melted down they went. John was also aware of this possibility and was adamant that his four-wheel be retrieved. I agreed. I was also afraid that if we doubled up any more it would put added strain on Eric's bent runners. After listening to my reasoning Eric finally agreed. Now I just hoped we could safely lift the machine out of the watery edge.

John and I moved carefully onto the thinner ice. Slowly we lifted the machine enough to push it onto solid ice. SUCCESS!! Once again we were on our way!

Eric decided to stay in the lead. He handed John a rope with instructions that if he broke through the ice we were to stop and throw him the rope. My only thought was, *Boy, isn't that reassuring*!

I put John in front of me. I wanted to keep him in my sight to make sure he didn't break through the ice again or get stuck in another snowdrift. Then we attempted to follow directly behind Eric. All too soon it was totally dark.

Now another problem presented itself. The tide had come in and the ice was covered with water. Thin layers of ice had formed just under the water and John's back wheels kept breaking through. Again and again I jumped off my machine to run up and help John lift the four-wheeler out of the ice, praying that we were over solid river ice and not a section of open water with just a thin layer of ice covering it. Then we would hurry to catch up to Eric. Sometimes we could barely see his taillight. In our haste I hoped we were staying far enough from the river's edge and the open water we'd seen on the way to Bethel. Finally, after what seemed like forever, we got out of the overflow water and on to solid ice.

Though all of this Anne had remained silent, probably because she realized the danger. She rode in front of me holding onto my upper arms. Going through the overflow I felt her hands clinching my arms. Once we hit solid ice her hands relaxed and she looked up at me, "Is there any more water, Mommy?"

"We are probably out of it now," I answered as I tried to reassure not only her but also myself. I hoped I was correct. I also said a little prayer and then promised, "...Lord, if I make it out of this I'll never work in the villages again!"

About that time we rounded a bend in the river and saw the village lights. I could have cried I was so relieved but knew we still had one more hurdle. A slew entered the Kuskokwim River right at the village. It was dangerous crossing if you missed the trail. About that time we saw lights coming toward us and within a few minutes we met. It was Don, Ed, the maintenance man, and Art, a worker who was helping remodel the school. They had come to search for us when we didn't return before dark.

They led us safely through the slew and into the village. What a relief when we finally reached home. I decided right then I'd never travel again when the natives said it wasn't yet time.

Don and Ed felt bad that they hadn't waited for us and Art was disgusted with the whole crew for putting the kids and me at risk by their arguing. He told me that whenever he went into Bethel I'd be welcome to go along.

The next day the weather warmed up melting more ice. Now no one could travel on the river. I wondered what was happening to John's gas and the school's sled. Someone might have stolen them or they could have broken through the ice in this warm weather and be at the bottom of the slew. These scenarios kept going through my mind. But a week later when Eric and John were finally able to travel the river they found the sled with the gas just where we had left it. John hooked up the sled and pulled his gas safely home.

In early December we had a warm spell and were unable to travel. We heard about several snow machines and three-wheelers that had gone through the ice. After our own experience, I preferred to stay home. One episode was enough and next time we might not be so lucky.

John, being the entrepreneur he was, decided to start a rocket club. He got several kids involved. They held bake sales to earn money to purchase their rockets. They spent a lot of time on the hobby when they couldn't be out hunting. It turned out to be a tremendous success.

That year I brought a Colecovision to go with the children's video games. I also ordered a number of videos for them for Christmas presents. During Christmas vacation we did little but watch videos and play games. Our favorite movies were "Annie" and "Grease." I wasn't totally happy with the "Grease" video for the younger kids, but before we left that spring I could recite most of it line by line I had watched it so often.

The mail came in on time and as usual Theresa sent us goodies. She was so faithful about sending surprises, especially chocolate, that I was getting a reputation as the local "choclaholic." The kids were super about writing her thank you notes, as they sure didn't want to dissuade her from sending more. We could many times tell the holiday by the shape of her gifts!

By now Anne was quite good at speaking Yupik. When she talked on the phone with her friends I had no idea what the discussion was about. This concerned me at times.

Several weeks after our memorable trip to Bethel, Art stopped by and asked, "Would you like to fly into Bethel with me to get groceries while I get the supplies I need?"

"Sure. We always need groceries and they're cheaper in Bethel," I responded.

We chartered in Saturday afternoon, got the supplies we each needed and went back to the airport. There we were told that no planes were flying from the airport because the fog was settling in, but since Napakiak was so close we might be able to get one of the pilots flying off the river to run us home. Quickly we drove to the river and found a pilot who was sure he could make it by flying under the fog. We loaded our supplies, boarded, and were on our way. The pilot skimmed along just above the ground and under the lowering fog, made a quick landing at Napakiak to drop us off, and headed back into Bethel. He must have barely made it because by the time we'd walked into the village the fog had settled to the ground.

It was a couple months later when Art said he had to go into Bethel again, but since the river was in such good traveling condition he was driving the pickup. It was a beautiful day and I thought that it would be a nice break from the village—and as usual, I could always use the groceries.

We headed out. The river was in great shape for traveling. As we neared Bethel though, I noticed we were passing more and more snowdrifts on each side of the pickup. Suddenly there was one directly in front of us. "We'd better slow down and try to get around that drift!" I urgently suggested.

"Oh, I think we can make it through," Art countered as he gunned the motor. Well, we didn't make it. We were jammed tight into that drift! "No problem," said Art as he hopped out to look over the situation. He had a shovel in the back of the pickup and began trying to dig us out. Unfortunately the drift in front stretched out for some distance. There was no way we could get out that way, and we were up to the bottom of the doors on the sides of the pickup.

After thirty to forty minutes of work we were still stuck deep in the drift when a car appeared. It held several native men from a neighboring village. They stopped, got out and walked slowly around the pickup to look over the situation. Then one of them approached Art and asked in amazement, "What were you trying to do?"

"I thought I could make it through the drift," Art replied.

The man just shook his head. They got shovels from their vehicle and soon had us on our way with the suggestion that we go AROUND any future drifts. Art was more careful to follow the marked trail after that and we made it in and out of Bethel with no more problems.

For most of January and early February the weather was so bad that we did little traveling. The absolute temperature stayed from about +5° to -30° but the wind chill stayed from -30° to -70° and it was just too unpredictable to take chances and go too far from the village.

John was on the wrestling team and gone almost every weekend for tournaments in neighboring villages. Anne was in band and one weekend they flew to Kwig for a band concert. As John and Shi-Ming were also gone that weekend, I couldn't believe I had two days all to myself!

Unfortunately, when Anne returned she had a frostbitten ear. It was red and blistery. I warmed it slowly for about an hour until it finally began to thaw and feel better. It seems they had to walk from the school to the airport, which was at least a half-mile. Then they had to wait in the bitter cold for the plane. I was glad they had flown on a twin otter, which is a small twin-engine prop plane. With so many kids and their instruments, it was nice having them on a much larger and safer plane than the regular bush plane.

About this time Kathy and I decided we needed to get something done to our hair so we made appointments in Bethel. The weather turned cold and there wasn't enough snow on the river to ride the snow machines, so we changed our appointments for the next weekend. Once again the weather was bad. Kathy suggested sharing a charter. Since I was tired of staying in the village I agreed. We chartered in, had our hair done, picked up some groceries and chartered back. When we returned we decided that had been our "once only" trip because the charters were $100 each way and our hairdos cost close to $100 each. That added up to a $200 hairdo for each of us. Oh well, you have to do something crazy once in a while!

The weather turned nice so a number of us decided to have a "girl's day out." There were three machines and six women. The river was frozen solid as we headed out. There was only one problem—no snow covered the ice, and we needed snow for traction. About halfway to Bethel the tracks on my smaller machine, carrying the double weight of Shi-Ming and me, started spinning and slipping and wouldn't move our machine.

We sat there debating what to do when we saw Don approaching in the school pickup. He was on his way back from school business in Bethel. Naturally he stopped and when he saw our predicament he started with the jokes about "women's ability to travel alone."

Me and my big mouth! I smarted back at which point he suggested that maybe we could get ourselves out of this mess. Quickly I retracted my statement. (At least until he could get us home!) He laughed as he suggested taking Shi-Ming back with him and following me to make sure I didn't have any more trouble. He had gotten what he wanted; a rise from me!

That year was not the best for snow machine travel but many times, weather permitting and no sick kids, for entertainment Ed, Lanay, Don, all our kids and I would load up on Friday nights and head into Bethel for groceries and a hamburger at the Kuskokwim Inn.

We'd put all the kids at one table and us at another. Our orders were usually pretty much the same each time, so one evening when Denny strayed from his usual order, the waitress came to the adult table to check it out. She explained to his dad that Denny had ordered steak and lobster. Ed calmly replied,

"Oh, in English that means hamburger and milkshake!" We all got quite a laugh out of that order.

After eating we would go to the grocery store, get our supplies, load up and head home. I rode my snow machine, John drove the four-wheeler, Don rode his snow machine pulling a sled for whatever we brought back, and Ed would ride his snow machine and pull a big sled with Lanay and the kids. Lanay would sit in the sled with her three kids and Anne around her. In that sled with solid sides and all covered with blankets, they rode nice and cozy, singing songs and having a great time.

As it was only twelve river miles to Bethel, we usually made it in thirty to forty minutes when pulling the sleds. On the way back it usually took longer. Invariably someone would stop and wave us down in order to make a profound statement such as, "What a beautiful moon out tonight!" We would all agree, then run and give Ed's big sled a shove to get him going as the runners heated up going down the river and usually froze into the ice when we stopped. Once he was free and moving the rest of us would jump back on our machines and head on home until someone else waved us down with another profound statement.

It got to be a game to see who could come up with something worthy enough to cause everyone to stop. On one such trip I stopped everyone to remark that it looked like the river had been graded. We all laughed, but as we neared Napakiak we were amazed to see a road grader just outside the village. Sure enough, the river had actually been graded!

One evening about dusk, after an especially frustrating day, I took the snow machine out for a ride to clear the cobwebs from my mind. I followed a little used trail to the river's edge, parked the machine and sat there for some time lost in my own thoughts. It was a beautiful, clear night. The soft glow of the full moon outlined mountains far to the south. The quiet was so complete you could almost hear the blood slowly coursing through your veins. The intense silence and the immenseness of the tundra filled me with an awe that made me wonder if it were scenes and feelings such as I was experiencing that kept the Eskimos from leaving that harsh, cold environment.

By the middle of April there was bad weather again. It would oscillate from a minus 30° wind-chill to 0°. Our neighbor, Cindy, started wearing shorts. We kidded her and told her we didn't think she was convincing Mother Nature. Actually, it was quite a common practice in the villages for the kids to start wearing shorts when the temperature reached above freezing. To them that was spring. But this wasn't even close to +32 degrees!

John spent a lot of his time hunting with Eric when he was home. On one trip he and Eric came across some overflow water. Thinking they could jump it with their machines they gave it a try. John wound up wet to his knees and by the time he got home he was solid ice. I had to thaw out his laces to get his boots off and then literally *pry* his pants off, as they were stiff with ice. It took him a while to thaw out but he had no lasting effects from this adventure.

For all of his trips and problems those two years, the worst thing he got was a frozen little finger from one of his earlier trips to Bethel. After that, whenever it got cold, it would bother him but it certainly didn't stop or slow him down. It was after that experience we learned to double up on the gloves with a thin pair under good, warm heavy ones.

This is John's story:

> One of the first things you learn in Alaska about bush travel is the danger of overflow. Close enough to the ocean, the rivers rise and fall with the tides. The center of the rivers could be frozen deep enough to land a plane, or drive a snowmobile, car or even a truck on. (Military vehicles were occasionally seen traveling the river.) However, when the river rose, the water could come out from under the edges extending further up each bank. At an average of -10° with a wind chill, it could quickly freeze over a layer up to an inch thick. The water would recede, coming back the next day under the 'shell' that had been created the day before.

If no new snow fell this hazard, often called 'black ice', was pretty easy to spot for the dark look created by the water under the thin ice.

Falling through the ice and getting wet was only half the problem. On a snowmobile or walking you also ran the risk of sliding under the thicker ice and being swept into the freezing river. Should you fall through and then get out any distance from the village you risk hypothermia, frostbite and the possibility of losing body parts when they thawed out.

Then there was 'gray snow'. Grey snow was snow that falls on the overflow ice, in affect hiding the danger. Someone who knows what to look for avoids this gray snow by going around it or if it is a short patch you can speed up and sort of hydroplane across it to the thicker ice. This is an educated guess you make from personal experience and learning from others. Even as young as I was, I became good at 'reading the river', and getting on and off without problems.

The whites new to the bush, bold to travel with little or no knowledge of the land, would often end up getting themselves, and occasionally others, in trouble. On a day trip with a friend, who also happened to be my science teacher, and his visiting friend from the lower forty-eight started out well enough. We were taking him out hunting to give him the total 'bush' experience.

Having only gotten a couple of ptarmigan, we headed down river to an area Eric and I knew to be good for both birds and rabbits. Going single file on our machines, we were moving at the edge of the river—Eric in the lead, me behind and his friend bringing up the rear. We were cruising easily along, probably doing fifteen to twenty mph when I suddenly saw Eric goose it and shoot ahead as we approached a slew entering the river. A slew is a smaller waterway usually less than fifty feet across and there were many entering the Kuskokwim. I saw the gray snow just as Eric hit the edge but fortunately he had enough time and speed that he neatly hydroplaned across to the heavier ice leaving a broken waterway in his path.

"Naturally I slowed to see where I should approach or possibly turn around and 'plane' cross further down when

I realized his friend had not noticed nor had paid attention to what was going on and was about to smash into the back of my machine and quite possibly sliding me into the now open water. Quickly I turned slightly and gunned it, trying to plane across next to where Eric had gone. But the ice was too weak from his path and less than half way across I broke through, the front of my machine slamming into the solid ice. My snowmobile was in water and I was wet to my knees. Instantly I hopped up and stood on my seat, the motor struggling to keep going as it was partially submerged in water. As it gurgled reluctantly, my shotgun fell away into the water. My first reaction was to shake off my glove and grab the gun before it sank.

"Our novice tag-along, realizing the danger too late, tried to turn away and slid part way into the water nearly tipping over his machine in a sudden effort to avoid the overflow. Fortunately his snowmobile stopped in less than six inches of water. He jumped back to the dry bank in a panic but reluctantly got back on his machine after a minute of coaxing and drove it out of the shallow depths.

"I, on the other hand, was stranded. Snowmobiles have no reverse. The front of my machine was against the solid ice with the front skis under the thick ice. After trying in vain to pull it up on the thick ice Eric and I used a short piece of rope to pull it back towards land just far enough to free the skis. Then we lifted them straight up and secured them to the back of Eric's snow machine. I jumped to the solid ice and our visitor was instructed to cross the slew a little further down river and come up by Eric's machine which he did in short order. It took all three of us, including the power of Eric's machine, to get my waterlogged machine out and up on the safe ice.

"By that time my boots were frozen and I had the icy needles of frostbite attacking both feet. I had to wait nearly another ten minutes while Eric tried and tried to get my snow machine started as it had 'died' while getting it to safe ice. Finally a miracle happened and it started—at least enough to travel under its own power and we immediately headed back to the village.

"Luckily we were only about ten miles out and got there in

short order. But that was long enough though and my boots had to be thawed to get them off my feet. My two smallest toes on my left foot were frostbitten. Fortunately the only damage to them was what looked and felt like a second-degree burn on that foot.

"Our guest learned quickly the harsh realities of the beautiful, but powerful, bush country of Alaska."

As the year progressed so did the pain in my leg and foot. It wasn't long before I was walking on tiptoe, as I could no longer put my heel down and use any weight. When I was seated working with the children I would prop my leg up on a small garbage can we had in the classroom. One day Don came in and noticed my leg propped up. He asked me about it. I told him it relieved the pain. He offered to have the high school shop class build me something that would be more comfortable. I declined, as I didn't think that would look too good, although it probably would have looked better than the garbage can!

After several trips to Bethel regarding my foot, I was set up with a specialist in Anchorage. The Bethel doctors were hesitant to try surgery. They said that many times it wouldn't heal properly and could affect my walking the rest of my life. As I couldn't walk correctly now I didn't see how it could be much worse!

Whenever possible I took the snow machine to Bethel for my doctor's appointments, but once when the weather was bad I caught the taxi. I quickly found out that wasn't necessarily the best way to go. After my doctor's appointment I went directly to the grocery store to wait for the return trip. When the taxi finally showed up there were ten of us waiting and only room for six. Thank goodness the men were gentlemen and the women were allowed to load first. Some of the men had to wait in Bethel for another way home.

There were never any guarantees with that taxi. He made one trip and took whoever was waiting when he felt like leaving. On one of John's taxi trips to Bethel he was left and had to spend the night with Shi-Ming and her husband, then catch a ride out the next day. Of course he didn't mind at all!

On one of my many trips to the doctors in Bethel I took John with me. I rode my snow machine and he rode his four-wheeler. There was always something of a contest to see who could make it into, or home from, Bethel in the best time. That day was perfect for traveling and as we started home I had a desire for speed. I put the "pedal to the metal" and we made it home in under fifteen minutes, which I was sure was a record. When we got off the machines John was annoyed and asked, "What were you trying to do? I could hardly keep up with you!"

I told him how fast we made it home and he was not to tell Don or Ed. I certainly didn't want one of them to get hurt trying to beat our time just because we had teased them about it. I guess John never did tell because nothing was ever said about our speedy trip.

I flew into Anchorage in March to see a specialist about my foot. The X-rays showed a large heal cyst. It was decided that surgery was the only option. We set it up for the day after school let out so I could have it taken care of on my way home. The doctors told me it probably wasn't cancerous, but they wouldn't know for sure until after the operation.

After returning to the village I worried about my upcoming operation. If it turned out to be cancer, that it would mean flights to Anchorage for treatment. Those flights would be costly and what would I do about the children? I was fortunate to have both Ed and Lanay and Eric and Kathy to help with the kids but was worried about what would happen if I really got sick. Also, I thought about the promise I made to leave the village if I got home from that horrible trip to Bethel in the fall.

I had a good friend who was a superintendent and had told me to call him if I ever decided to come back to the lower forty-eight to teach. After much deliberation, I decided it was now time to make that call. As luck would have it he was anticipating an opening in his third grade and would love for me to come, but I had to interview with the grade school principal, as I would actually be working for him. Not wasting any time, I called the principal and scheduled an interview for a couple of weeks after arriving in Oregon. That would give my foot time to partially heal before making the trip.

Those decisions having been made, I once again began packing. I packed the majority of our belongings so that if I came back in the summer it wouldn't take long to finish.

There were twelve gussaks in the village. The day school let out eleven of us were lined up along the runway waiting for our charters within an hour of release time. Don's contract lasted for several more weeks.

The first charter came for Lois and her husband. It put down on the runway and skidded off to one side. My first thought was, *This is not a good sign.* The pilot jumped out and with help from the guys soon had the plane back on the runway. Lois and her husband loaded up and flew off to Bethel. I was a little apprehensive at this point, but as there was no other way out of the village we had little choice but to fly out when our plane arrived. We had ordered a larger plane so several of us could share the cost. Our charter was late, but when it did arrive it landed with no trouble. We flew to Bethel; then on to Anchorage that same day. There we parted company. Ed, Lanay and family flew to Missouri. Since Kathy and Eric were going to Oregon they agreed to take John and Anne with them as far as Portland. I arranged for Dad to drive to Portland, meet the kids at the airport and take them to my brothers to await my arrival.

After everyone left I checked into the hospital. The next day the huge cyst was removed from my heel. The doctor said the cyst was about the size of a golf ball, but flat on one side. He made the incision on the side of my foot hoping that it wouldn't hinder my walking. He also explained that there might never be much feeling on the inside section of my heel so I should be especially careful not to injure it.

I was only in the hospital one night after the surgery. The next day a friend drove me to the airport. With the help of crutches and a wheelchair, I too boarded a plane for Portland. Thoughtfully, they put me in the front row of the airplane so I would have more legroom. Three hours later I was reunited with my children.

About ten days later and still on crutches, I loaded John and Anne and drove to Waterville, Washington, for my interview. As I drove up the five-mile hill out of Wenatchee I thought, *This is almost as isolated as the villages.* For some reason I was close to tears over the thought that I might be isolated again. Then I calmed down and realized that Wenatchee was only twenty miles away, and I could actually *drive* down almost any time I wanted.

My interview went well and I was offered a position teaching third grade, which I accepted. That week I also learned that my growth had not been cancerous.

As soon as my foot was heeled enough for me to get off the crutches, I purchased a round trip ticket to Napakiak. The first story I heard when I arrived in the village was about a woman whose snow machine had gone through the ice during the winter. Her body had washed up on the shore near Napakiak only a couple of days before my arrival. All I could think of was, *That could have been my entire family!*

I arrived late in the day and spent time lining up transportation to get my boxes to the post office the next morning. The maintenance man decided it would be okay to use the school truck since I was still an employee. Then I tackled the balance of the packing. Thankfully I had packed almost everything. After a while I noticed I was getting extremely tired. The electricity to my house had been cut off for the summer so I was working by daylight. When I looked at my watch I was shocked to see it was almost 2:00 a.m. and I could still see well enough to pack. But I was so tired I decided to sleep for a few hours before finishing.

Early next morning I was ready to go. With the help of the maintenance man I loaded my belongings into the truck. He drove me the short distance to the post office and helped me carry everything inside. We weighed box after box. The postal lady warned me that all my belongings would not be sent out together, as the mail plane wouldn't be able to carry so many boxes at one time. I told her that was fine, and we finished up the task.

Next, I had to catch the plane back to Bethel where I went to the LKSD offices and filled out my resignation papers. After that I returned to the airport to catch my flight to Anchorage. As the plane rose over the tundra, I silently said my final goodbye to the villages of Western Alaska.

Epilogue

One of the things I observed during the three years I spent in the Western Alaskan villages, is that we who don't live there and haven't experienced the vagaries of the elements become somewhat cocky. Looking back at our traumatic experience, I see there was *no* excuse for my risking the lives of my children and myself because of an impatience to do what we wanted to do. The next year I heard that Don lost his snow machine, and almost his life, when he went through weak ice in his attempt to reach Bethel before the river was sufficiently frozen.

The natives run on their own time, and it is closely related to "ifs" and "maybes," many times pronounced ma-a-a be-e-e. They didn't plan and execute. They went "if" the tide came in or "if" the planes flew. Then "maybe" they would go to Bethel. Their patience and slower lifestyle must be what allows them to continue to exist in the harsh environment of the tundra.